Homework Talk!

The Art of Effective Communication About Your Child's Homework

Cheli Cerra, M.Ed. & Ruth Jacoby, Ed.D.

JOSSEY-BASS
A Wiley Imprint
www.josseybass.com

Published by Jossey-Bass
A Wiley Imprint
989 Market Street, San Francisco, CA 94103-1741   www.josseybass.com

Jossey-Bass books and products are available through most bookstores. To contact Jossey-
Bass directly call our Customer Care Department within the U.S. at 800-956-7739, outside the
U.S. at 317-572-3986, or fax 317-572-4002.

Jossey-Bass also publishes its books in a variety of electronic formats. Some content that
appears in print may not be available in electronic books.

ISBN 13: 978-0-7879-8273-7
ISBN 10: 0-7879-8273-3

Printed in the United States of America
FIRST EDITION

PB Printing   10 9 8 7 6 5 4 3 2 1

The Buzz About Homework Talk!

"Homework is a constant battle for many families. It's reassuring to know how many families will benefit from the proven, practical information and easy-to-implement suggestions in Homework Talk! By using this information many frustrated students will finally be able to experience the 'joy of learning!'"

Lisa Simmons
Director, Ideal Lives Inclusion & Advocacy Center

"Homework Talk! *is a wonderful source for parents that makes homework time helpful and not hurtful. This book gives parents a workable, realistic schedule and helps build communication between home and school.*"

Dina Miller, *M.Ed.*
School Principal and Parent

"The tips and techniques in Homework Talk! *will definitely be beneficial for my parents. This book gets students focused and organized when doing homework assignments. One key factor that I have taken from this book is that it is essential for the parent to be part of the homework process.*"

Shirrie Barany
Exceptional Child Specialist

To parents everywhere—
Happy homework!

Table of Contents

Preface

Homework—it's the eight-letter word that many parents dread, because it places special demands on a family. We know what it's like to have to hound your child to do homework. We appreciate how difficult it is to find time to work with your child on schoolwork. We understand what it is like to come home from work, exhausted, only to hear "Mom, I have a book report due and I forgot to. . . ."

We realize how busy you are, and the last thing we want this book to do is give you more "home" work. What we *do* want is to give you the knowledge and resources you need to make sure your child benefits from homework assignments that lead to school success. This book provides the essential tools, simply and quickly, that will help you help your child.

We have written this book to be accessible and easy to read. The snapshots you will find throughout reflect real-life situations parents face in dealing with homework. You will also find answers to common questions, such as: Why is homework important? What value does it bring to my child's education?

This book is only as effective as you make it. We hope that as you turn each page you will continue to learn and become a mentor to your child in his or her school success.

www.school-talk.com

INTRODUCTION
How to Use This Book

Just like you, we are parents who were concerned about homework when our own children were going through the grades. We understand how busy you are, and our intention is not to add more stress to your busy lives. In fact, it's our goal to accomplish just the opposite. We want to empower you with the essential knowledge and effective actions that will ensure your child is homework-savvy and a more successful student. Our goal in writing this book is to assist you in making homework a high-priority activity that involves family interaction and instills a lifelong love of learning.

We have organized this book in an easy-to-read format. Each of the five chapters focuses on an important aspect of homework and will increase your understanding of the value of homework. You will learn the importance of maintaining a schedule, acquire the ability to communicate with teachers and your child, and understand why homework is an important extension of the school day. Snapshots throughout the book provide real-life situations parents face with their children and their school when dealing with homework rituals. Each one is followed by strategies and tips for communicating effectively with your child and the school personnel and eliminating nightly homework battles. Worksheets, checklists, sample letters, and contracts that you will find throughout the book are designed to help you use what you have learned. At the end of each chapter we have added "Your Homework Assignment," intended for use by the parent, focusing on questions to ask, items to review, and tasks to complete. By using these tools, you will become confident that your child knows how to review and practice what she has learned, works independently, manages time well, and consistently meets deadlines.

Our ultimate goal is to give your child the positive "know-how" to achieve homework success. And you play a big part in that success. To better understand how your child learns, be sure to look at Appendix A: Secrets for a Smarter Child Revealed: Learning Styles.

With this book, you will be:

- *Proactive:* Become a take-charge parent and a can-doer, working in your child's best interest. Seek assistance and advice from the school as soon as problems arise. Don't wait.

- *O*rganized: Set up a homework schedule and stick to it. Have homework contracts handy if you decide this will help your child take on the homework responsibilities. Be ready to celebrate the successes and conquer the challenges.
- *W*ell-prepared: Set up an environment at home that shows your child homework is a top priority. Set an example by reading and writing, and encourage visits to museums and libraries. Decrease the television time and telephone usage and play educational games.
- *E*ffective: Communication is the key. Be prepared to telephone, write notes, and/or e-mail the school as problems arise. Waiting for any length of time can jeopardize progress.

Be ready to communicate with your child the plans you have laid out and remind him that the more completed homework assignments he turns in, the better his school grades and scores on standardized tests will be.

- *R*eflective: The parent "homework assignments" at the end of the chapter will help you review, reflect on, and plan winning strategies.

Now you'll have the POWER to create smooth-running and hassle-free nights where homework assignments are effectively completed without complaints and reminders.

www.school-talk.com

Try This Out: Your First Homework Assignment

Take the following Homework Communication Assessment. Step 1 will help you determine your level of comfort in speaking with school staff when difficult situations arise at home with your child, target areas in which you need assistance, and recognize your strengths. Count up the number of "yes" answers, and then find the corresponding comments below. Keep the areas that were answered "no" as part of your top priorities, then move on to Step 2 and the final steps.

Homework Communication Assessment

Step 1: Circle "yes" or "no" to give the answer you find most appropriate.

Yes	No	1.	I am comfortable speaking with teachers.
Yes	No	2.	I listen more than I talk.
Yes	No	3.	I am comfortable requesting a conference with the teacher.
Yes	No	4.	I am at ease when meeting with the school staff.
Yes	No	5.	I do not believe I know more than the teachers do.
Yes	No	6.	I contact teachers immediately when my child has difficulty with or takes too long to complete homework assignments.
Yes	No	7.	I like to have teacher talks.
Yes	No	8.	I speak with my child about homework assignments daily.
Yes	No	9.	I respect the teacher's homework policies.
Yes	No	10.	I have a homework policy for my child that stresses the importance of having a schedule and rules to follow for completing homework successfully and handing it in on time.

Tally the number of "yes" answers. If you scored:

8 or higher: You are on your way to becoming an effective communicator.

6 to 8: You may want to read carefully those snapshots addressing areas in which you are weak and practice the tips and techniques. The other snapshots may give you further insight and communication skills to improve your conversational style and homework knowledge.

5 or under: You will want to read all the chapters and snapshots. Practice the techniques, asking friends and family to assist you.

Step 2: Visualize a perfect night where there are no complaints about homework, everyone eats dinner at the same time, and there is even time for reading and leisure activities. Can this happen for your family? Yes it can! Take a few minutes and follow these easy steps:

   a. Write down everything you would like to accomplish to have things go smoothly in your home every night.

   b. In order of importance, put a number in front of each goal.

   c. Read the snapshots detailed in the book that address those areas where you need assistance.

   d. Try out the tips and strategies suggested.

   e. Make the goals a reality and they will be part of your nightly ritual. Homework will no longer be a struggle, but an enriching and rewarding experience that will foster parent-child quality time.

Step 3: To increase your homework savvy, fill out the following survey and review how you did. It will give you insight and help guide you through your role in the nightly homework rituals.

Parent Homework Survey

Circle "yes" or "no" to see how you view your role in the nightly homework process.

Yes No 1. Do you inform the teacher immediately when your child does not have the skills to complete an assignment?

Yes No 2. Do you check completed homework to see if it is done correctly?

Yes No 3. Do you know the teacher's homework policies?

Yes No 4. Are you working with your child on homework as she needs it?

Yes No 5. Do you have a homework schedule and policy in your home?

Yes No 6. Do you have a quiet area in your home for doing homework?

Yes No 7. Do you reward homework successes?

Yes No 8. Does your child know that you feel homework is the most important extension of school?

Yes No 9. Do you have fellow classmates' phone numbers or the teacher's e-mail address in case your child forgets his homework journal?

Yes No 10. Are you conferencing with the teacher when you feel there is too much homework or the assignments are too easy?

Yes No 11. Do you encourage your child to ask for assistance in school and at home?

Yes No 12. Do you give consequences for incomplete homework papers and are you consistent with those consequences?

Yes No 13. Do you have a set schedule for homework for those days your child has no outside activities and an alternative schedule for those days your child has afterschool commitments?

Yes No 14. Do you conference with the teacher to come up with a plan to fix homework problems? Do you follow up with the school? Do you carry out the plan?

Tally the number of "yes" answers. If you scored:

12 or higher: You have a handle on how to assist with homework.

9, 10, or 11: You need to review some of your homework policies and make adjustments to increase your child's homework success.

8 or under: Read the sections in the book that address how you can lend a hand in increasing your child's homework accomplishments.

Step 4: Use the following Monthly Self-Evaluation to help you keep on track. By reviewing and answering these questions each month, you will see where you need to make adjustments.

Monthly Self-Evaluation

Answer these questions at the end of each month.

1. What are my child's homework struggles? What are my child's homework successes?

2. What tip can I use to change a bad homework habit into an accomplishment?

   a. Create a schedule.

   b. Check planner/journal nightly to see if assignment was completed.

   c. Assist with skills when needed.

   d. Give rewards for homework successes.

   e. Be consistent with consequences for incomplete assignments or for not doing homework.

   f. Make homework a top priority.

   g. Other.

3. How can I inspire my child?

   a. Am I asking the teacher for assistance?

   b. Am I setting high expectations for my child?

   c. Am I communicating to my child that doing homework will increase her grades and success on all tests?

   d. Am I insisting my child do his best at all times?

Step 5: Appendix C will introduce you and your family to fun activities that will enrich family time while increasing your child's higher-order thinking skills. For example, you can designate a game night, when television and telephone are shut off and family members can gather and be involved together. Taking part in the activities found on the back pages can turn a run-of-the-mill evening or weekend into a fun-filled learning experience.

CHAPTER ONE
Why Homework?

"With each new day, there is a new lesson. . . . It prepares us for what is yet to come!"
E. Skiver

What exactly is homework and why should your child do it? Does homework really have any educational value or is it just busywork? What is the purpose of homework? Is it simply a way for the teacher to show that she's doing her job? Does it serve to make the school seem more academic and prestigious?

Although you do your best to comply with homework demands, you no doubt find that homework cuts into your family time. You may wonder whether homework is worth the demands and stress it can put on families.

In this chapter we will address the importance of homework, and how homework provides the skills that lay the foundation your child will need to achieve academic success. Research tells us that children who consistently do homework have better school grades and test scores. Homework also provides a great opportunity for you to assist your child in becoming successful, and it allows you to keep on track with what your child is learning in school.

This chapter will address:

- Why a child should do homework
- The educational value of homework
- How homework increases school success
- How homework is an extension of the school day

www.school-talk.com

Snapshot #1:

Why Should My Child Do Homework?

It seems like our family is always short on time. Between our jobs and juggling all the kids' activities, we don't have time for family meals, much less hours to spend working on homework each night. My child is an excellent student, goes to school each day, and is attentive in class. I don't want my child to have to do homework. What should I do?

Working with your child and the school brings positive results.

Many studies have found that homework is effective in improving academic skills and achievement, especially at the middle and high school levels. However, acquiring self-discipline and the habit of doing homework must be developed at the elementary level.

As a parent, you will do your child a great favor if you understand the benefits of homework and support your child in making time to complete home assignments.

Tip : In today's world, where many parents have demanding jobs and children join in multiple activities, it's difficult to make the time for homework. However, homework can be extremely valuable and is assigned for several reasons.

First, in a classroom with dozens of students, a teacher might not have the opportunity to see whether each child has understood a concept. By doing homework, a student has the chance to analyze, practice, and then master the concept on his own.

Second, think about the times you've been given a fact or an idea and you say, "I need time to think about that." The same is true for many of the theories put forward during the school day. Children may need time away from classroom distractions to process an idea or may simply need to read more about it at their own pace.

Third, studies show that doing a reasonable amount of homework DOES positively affect a child's ability level—as well as class rank.

Fourth, having a homework regimen teaches a student self-discipline and study skills.

21

Snapshot #2:

Does Homework Have Any Educational Value or Is It Just Busywork?

Recently, I watched a show on television about the pressures on today's kids. Many of these kids talked about the stress of doing a lot of homework. My son keeps complaining that his homework is the same stuff they did in school. I feel that my son has to do homework that doesn't have any educational value. What should I do?

It's important to note, however, that the most educational value comes from homework that is not just "busywork," but relevant to the student in the "real world." A child's interest and understanding vastly improve when homework is both challenging and "real world–based" rather than simple rote learning or dry theory.

Tip : Homework does have educational value! Multiple studies have shown that doing homework benefits a child in many ways. However, since you have a concern, talk with your son and schedule a conference with the teacher to discuss your feelings.

You may find out that homework gives a child a chance to "think" about things that were presented during a lesson but weren't discussed in depth, that homework allows a child to practice with and manipulate the information. We all know that it's a far different thing to watch and listen to someone else do something than to "do it ourselves." We also know that most of us weren't born being able to do math or write paragraphs. Some skills are vastly improved with repeated exposure and practice. Homework has been proven to significantly raise ability levels, achievement scores, and class rankings. In addition, homework offers you the opportunity to be involved with your son's education, and in many cases, to offer insights on how the subject matter could be applied in practical, realistic situations. In doing so, you help your son see the value of what he's learning.

Snapshot #3:

My Preschool-Age Son Is Already Concerned About Homework. What Should I Say to Him?

Every day after she arrives home from school, my daughter, who is a sixth-grader, complains about having to do her homework. My four-year-old son sees this and it's causing him some concern. The other day he asked me, "Mom, what is homework? Is it bad?" What should I do?

Tip: Be both honest and positive. Tell your young son that homework is a part of going to school. Consider putting the concept into a situation he understands: If he plays T-ball and you practice batting and throwing with him in the yard, that's a kind of "homework." It's practice done "at home," not during game time, to improve his skills. Even though your workouts are at home and not in the ballpark, and you don't do them with other team members or his coach, point out that he still has fun doing them. And the more practice or "homework" he does, the better a player he becomes.

Show him how homework can be enjoyed. It's a chance to practice skills and gain confidence. Sometimes he practices T-ball at home because he doesn't get enough times at bat during practice sessions or games. The same is true with schoolwork. There may not be enough time to study all the subjects, have recess, and practice what he learned that day unless he "practices" it at home. Show him how you enjoy being with him and that homework, like practicing ball, can be either an activity you help him with or one he does by himself. Explain that the big leaguers—and all people who are successful—work hard to get where they are. By doing his homework, he can do well in school and be a real winner.

www.school-talk.com

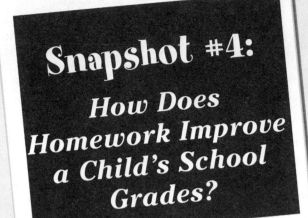

Snapshot #4:

How Does Homework Improve a Child's School Grades?

> *Children who regularly do homework develop study skills, self-discipline, and self-motivation—all factors that lead to success not just in school, but in life.*

My neighbor's daughter and my son are in the same class. My neighbor is constantly complaining that her daughter isn't doing well in school and that she takes hours to do her homework each night. My son, however, usually finishes his nightly homework within an hour and has good grades. Yesterday my neighbor came over, very upset, saying that homework is making her daughter fail. She wants me to sign a petition to stop homework. What should I do?

Tip : First, make your neighbor a cup of chamomile tea and let her talk. After she is done tell her that you understand her frustration and want to help her. If she is really angry at the teacher, ask whether she has ever talked with him about her feelings or has let the situation get out of control. The first step is to have your neighbor express her feelings to you. Once she's calmed down a bit and her feelings are under control, she needs to schedule a conference with the teacher. You may want to help her write a letter to the teacher stating her concerns or make a list of concerns she can take with her to the conference to stay focused. Help your neighbor understand that school success and homework go hand in hand. It's possible that homework is not the real issue. Her daughter may be having difficulty in school, which is being carried over at home through her homework.

How to Be Heard: Talking to Your Child's Teacher Effectively

The best way to approach any situation is to be prepared. When scheduling a parent-teacher conference, keep the following points in mind:

Before the Conference:
- Write down everything you want to discuss.
- Prioritize the list.
- Take the items from the list and make a statement out of each one. Follow up each statement with supporting evidence. Example: I am concerned that my child spends too much time on homework. On the average it is taking four hours a night.
- Look at all the items. If you have more than three items of concern, try to group together those that are similar. Remember: Less is more. Your concerns will have more of an impact if presented in a simple and concise way.
- Take the top three statements and follow up with a nonthreatening question. Example: How can we work together to make sure that my child is getting the best education possible?
- Be sure to take the time to think about something positive that the teacher has done for your child and tell her about it.

Key Points for a Successful Meeting

- Go in with a positive and cooperative attitude.
- Always be prepared.
- Be respectful and professional.
- Let the teacher know you support him, but also let him know that you want to make sure that your child's best interests are of primary importance.
- If you feel the conference is going nowhere, end on a positive note and schedule a meeting with the principal.

Snapshot #5:

My Son Is Starting to Struggle with Math

My son, who has just started struggling with math, repeatedly asks, "How is doing homework going to help anything?" I am at a loss. I want to help him understand the importance of homework in his ultimate success. What should I do?

Individual practice and repeated exposure to a subject through homework increases a child's ability in that subject.

Tip : Sit down and have a little heart-to-heart talk with your son. It's hard not to sympathize with him. Working on something that you struggle with is a difficult task. But it's also possible he is playing on your sympathy a little to get out of doing homework. (Let's face it. Kids are human and would probably rather have fun than sit down and do homework. Wouldn't we rather relax than do the laundry?)

Ask your son why he feels the way that he does. Listen to him and explain that "practice makes perfect!" Talk to your child's teacher, tell her how he is feeling, and ask for help and suggestions on what you can do at home to assist him. Tell your son that using your mind is like using any other muscle in your body. The more you work it, the better and stronger it gets. Tell him that whether it is playing an instrument, learning to swim, kicking a soccer ball, or learning long division, all skills take practice. The more he does it, the better he gets. Doing homework lets him spend more than just class time on mastering skills, and he gets to practice it on his own, at his own speed, in his own environment, with no one around to notice missteps or errors. Working through problems also helps him find out what step or part of the process he doesn't understand, giving him a place to start asking the teacher questions. You can also call to his attention the absolute necessity of math skills by talking about how you use math in everyday life. If the problem continues, talk to the teacher and ask if there is any tutoring available.

How Well Do You Know Your Child?

Take the following quiz:

1. What is your child's favorite subject in school?
2. What is your child's least favorite subject in school?
3. What is your child's favorite sport?
4. Who are your child's closest friends?
5. Do you spend at least fifteen minutes each day listening to your child, without any other distractions?

Sit down with your child and go over your answers. Talk to your child for at least fifteen minutes about what she likes best about school. Ask your child what subjects in school she is having a hard time with. The first step for success starts with positive thinking. Say something positive to your child.

Never, Ever Do Your Child's Homework!

It is late, you are tired, your child is cranky, and the assignment is far from finished. You are tempted, but WAIT! Don't give in!

Doing an assignment, research paper, or science project yourself can be tempting, especially if it is the eleventh hour. Helping your child with homework is very different from doing the homework for him. Parents can provide productive help by calling out spelling words or checking over math problems after the child has completed the work. You are teaching your child not only how to become smarter but also how to be successful, and a principle part of success is accepting responsibility. Homework is the responsibility of your child.

Snapshot #6:

How Does Homework Help a Child with Time Management?

Routine, routine, routine.

My daughter is eleven and a terrible procrastinator! No matter how much or how little homework she has, she always puts it off until the last minute and then must rush through it or stay up late to get it finished. What should I do?

Tip: The first step is to talk to your daughter to discover whether there's a reason she avoids homework. Is she overwhelmed by the sheer amount of it? Does she need a break immediately after school? Is there a television show that she is particularly fond of and doesn't want to miss? Finding out why she avoids homework and then helping her develop a schedule that fits her "clock" will make homework easier.

Teach her to manage time by breaking down homework into manageable blocks. For instance, have her work in twenty-minute intervals followed by a five-minute break. Follow the Daily Schedule plan shown here. Some visually oriented students benefit from seeing a schedule drawn out. Others acquire time-management skills when they are paired with external motivation. If your daughter sticks to a specified time-management plan and completes her homework before a deadline, then she can be rewarded with a treat or an extra half hour of television. Help her prioritize her work by doing the hardest homework first and saving the easiest parts for last.

Praise her when she finishes each assignment. Once she gets the hang of focusing for short periods of time and prioritizing her workload, she will complete the work more quickly, begin to dread it less, and consequently stop the procrastination.

Remember, homework can teach your child time-management skills that will serve her in high school, college, and beyond.

To make your child successful, you need to make sure he follows a routine. Balance is very important. Your child needs time to unwind and play. When your child comes home from school, what does he do? Does your child like to go outside and play, watch TV, or read? How does your child relax? Is your child involved in sports or other extracurricular activities? The best way for your child to follow a schedule is to get organized. Take a piece of paper and a pencil. Sit down with your child and map out his daily routine. You may want to have a regular schedule for the week (Monday through Friday) and one for the weekend (Saturday and Sunday).

Daily Schedule: Example #2

Time	Activity
7:00 A.M.	Wake up and get ready for school
7:30 A.M.	Breakfast
8:00 A.M.	Go to school
8:30 A.M.	School
3:30 P.M.	Get home from school
3:45 P.M.	Eat snack
4:00 P.M.	Soccer practice (Mon-Wed-Fri)
5:00 P.M.	Piano lessons (Tue-Thu)
6:00 P.M.	Dinner
7:00 P.M.	Homework
9:30 P.M.	Bedtime

Daily Schedule: Example #1

Time	Activity
7:00 A.M.	Wake up and get ready for school
7:30 A.M.	Breakfast
8:00 A.M.	Go to school
8:30 A.M.	School
3:30 P.M.	Get home from school
3:45 P.M.	Eat snack
4:00 P.M.	Homework
5:30 P.M.	Free time
6:30 P.M.	Dinner
7:45 P.M.	TV/computer time
9:30 P.M.	Bedtime

Daily Schedule: Example #3

(For the Working Parent)

Time	Activity
7:00 A.M.	Wake up and get ready for school
7:30 A.M.	Breakfast
8:00 A.M.	Go to school
8:30 A.M.	School
3:00–6:00 P.M.	Afterschool program
6:30 P.M.	Get home from school and finish homework
7:00 P.M.	Dinner
7:30 P.M.	Check and review homework
8:00 P.M.	TV/computer time
9:30 P.M.	Bedtime

Snapshot #7:

Why Is Homework Considered an Extension of the School Day?

As a parent, I am often frustrated by school officials who tell me that my child should have to do homework nightly. I firmly believe that work should be completed in the classroom and not sent home. I want to understand why teachers feel that doing homework is a necessary extension of the school day. What should I do?

Tip: Review the packet that most teachers send home the first day of school. It usually contains information about the school day and policies. Homework is one of those procedures the teacher likes to deal with right away so as a parent you will understand why it is given and how much to expect. You can further address homework guidelines at the open house. Teachers do understand that many parents today are battling the frustrations of a busy world and a harried family schedule. However, you need to understand teachers have a limited amount of time with their children and they too have pressures to cover all the material that needs to be dealt with in a limited amount of time. Educators often explain to parents that doing homework also allows them to see what their children are working on at school and how well they are doing in the subject matter, and provides a link between school, teacher, and child.

Homework also provides a way for a parent, student, and teacher to connect personally through feedback and comments on assignments, which, if done well, can contribute positively to a student's motivation.

Snapshot #8:
How Does Homework Benefit the Parent?

A t a recent PTA meeting, members of the board asked for ideas on how to get more parents involved. Many parents believe that being involved in their child's education is an activity only those people who don't have full-time jobs can enjoy. As PTA president, I want to promote the idea that parent participation in a child's learning is beneficial to the parent as well as the child. What should I do?

> *The most important person in a child's life is a parent.*

Tip : You are smart to be a proactive PTA president. By having the parents understand the importance of the home-school connection, the school will reach greater heights of success. Even if parents can't be volunteering in school, it doesn't mean they can't be actively involved in their child's academic life! One benefit both parents and children receive from homework is the ability to give and to get the parents' personal insight and practical experience about a subject. A child studying state history, for example, would benefit from hearing a parent's knowledge of ancestors who were early settlers. If a math lesson involves fractions, parents might point out real-world instances in which knowledge of fractions came in handy for them. Encouragement from a parent boosts the child's knowledge and appreciation of the parent. What parent doesn't like to seem helpful and smart in the eyes of a child?

Another perk for involved parents is an increased understanding of their child's personality and abilities. You might not have known your daughter has a fear of snakes if you hadn't been talking to her about her science lesson. Perhaps you didn't know that your son was the class mathematician until you monitored his homework. Knowing what lessons are covered in class also allows a parent to be proactive. If a child is struggling with a subject, a parent who knows what's being taught can help before it's too late. Finally, parents who know what's going on in the classroom will benefit by being prepared. They won't be surprised the night before a project is due with the agonized yell, "But I haven't even started!"

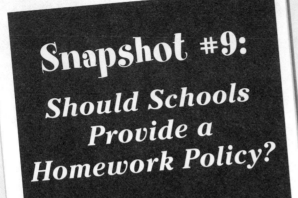

Snapshot #9:

Should Schools Provide a Homework Policy?

It's not always easy to get a universal answer when you are interviewing at your child's new school, so it may be best to ask these questions of your child's teacher.

Our family has just moved across the country. The previous school my child attended had a schoolwide policy on homework. Her new school does not. I expected the school to give me information and provide a homework policy. What should I do?

One accepted guideline is based on research gleaned from one hundred studies of homework compiled by Harris Cooper, a psychology professor at the University of Missouri. Cooper's guideline suggests ten to twenty minutes every night at first grade and then a ten-minute increase per each succeeding grade level.*

Tip : While some schools and school districts have developed an official homework policy, others have no universal approach to this age-old dilemma. Much controversy remains over the amount of homework to be assigned, the kind of assignments, the amount of parental involvement expected, and whether or not homework should be assigned at all. Your best bet is to schedule a conference with your child's teacher and ask the following questions:

- Are teachers expected to assign homework?
- Is there a guideline teachers follow about how many minutes of homework should be given to a student depending on age or grade level? Is there a homework-free weekend policy? (Some teachers feel that children need free time to spend with their families and friends.)

*Romesh Ratnesar, "The Homework Ate My Family," *Time,* Jan. 25, 1999, p. 54.

32

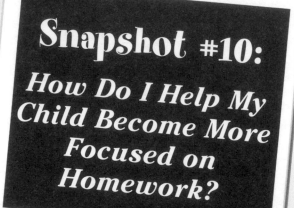

Snapshot #10:
How Do I Help My Child Become More Focused on Homework?

My son is just not doing his homework. No matter what I try, I can't seem to get him to stay focused. I often find him doodling or singing to himself or just staring off into space. He also uses any excuse to stop working—jumping up to get a glass of water, answer the phone, sharpen his pencil, pet the dog, whatever distraction he can think of. I want to help him concentrate. What should I do?

Tip: Make sure that your son has a break after school, allowing him to burn off some energy before getting down to business. Also, setting aside the same time each day to do homework will help him develop the "homework habit." Find a special place for him to do homework, whether it's a desk in his bedroom or a designated area of the kitchen. The area should be quiet, free from distractions, and comfortable. (Let the child make the space his own by picking out special pencil holders, putting up a bulletin board, or having his favorite accessories handy.) Talk to him about what he's studying in school, and then help him look over his homework. Ask him which assignment is hardest and have him do that first. Teach him to break up each assignment into smaller parts. For instance, if he has to answer twenty questions, tell him that after he completes the first ten, he can get up and have a cookie, making sure he understands that after the cookie, he has to return to finish the next ten problems. After every half hour, allow a ten-minute "fun" break. As often as possible, show him how what he's working on is used in real life. Finally, after he's done his homework, review it with him, praising him for his hard work, and then allow him to do something he enjoys. You might consider using a calendar to help keep track of his assignments and due dates. Learning how to do homework teaches a child how to stay more focused on all projects and tasks in the future.

Does your child's mind tend to wander? Does he have a hard time focusing?

Being a dreamer is a positive quality of creative minds. Children who love to daydream and are creative have a special gift and parents and teachers must encourage them to keep this unique gift alive. HOWEVER, there is a time and place for creative activity.

How do you help your creative, mind-wandering, daydreaming child focus?

Since this kind of child generally is not task-oriented, you can help by breaking down an assignment into smaller "bites." Example: Your child has to complete ten math problems. Get a timer and set it for ten minutes. Tell your child he has ten minutes to finish problem #1. When the timer goes off, check on your child. Then set the timer for the next "bite," and so on. Do this until all problems are finished. You can adjust the time you allot to fit the assignment and the age and the ability of your child. Breaking down the assignment into these manageable bite-size pieces will keep your child focused and moving forward through his homework.

Your Homework Assignment: Why Homework?

Directions: Now that you have completed Chapter One, take some time to answer the following questions. This is a short assignment that will act as a review and, we hope, increase your understanding of the key points.

1. Why is it important for your child to do homework?

2. List three things that homework can help your child with.

   a.

   b.

   c.

3. What is your child's homework routine?

4. How does homework help your child become a better student?

CHAPTER TWO
The Homework State of Mind

"I am neither especially clever, nor especially gifted. I am only very, very curious."
Albert Einstein

This chapter will explain how you can set an organizational tone for your child that leads to homework success as well as successes in later life. Specific suggestions, forms, and strategies are given on:

- Organizing a home learning environment.
- Incorporating homework into quality family time.
- Establishing schedules and routines that will keep everyone sane.
- Following up with both negative consequences and positive rewards.
- Teaching children how to keep a homework planner/journal, calendar, and folder. A planner—or journal—is a book that can be made using a notebook or is provided by the school. The child writes down daily assignments, tests, and project dates. There is a section for teacher and parent comments. Sometimes the preprinted ones provide an area for weekly spelling words and for parent signature. They are usually set up as weekly schedules.
- Encouraging students to communicate and listen in class and to take responsibility.

This chapter also provides tips on communicating effectively with the school, what assistance and resources you should look for from the school, and what the role of the teacher should be.

www.school-talk.com

Snapshot #11:

Doing Homework to Music Just Doesn't Work

One afternoon, I checked on my son, who was doing his homework in his bedroom. I found him sitting at his desk with his headphones on listening to his favorite pop music while reading a story and answering related questions. After completing that part of the assignment, he logged on to the computer to write a short report about the story's main character. While he seemed to take a long time to complete this, I was pleased at his doing the work without my assistance. He finally emerged from his room, said he had done all his homework and made all the corrections, and asked to go outside before dinner. I agreed, but first wanted to check his work. As I read what he'd written, I found an error. Instead of writing a short report about the main character, his report contained the words to a song he'd been listening to. It seemed he got distracted. What should I do?

Tip : Pop music is not the best music to listen to while doing homework. For some children this type of music can be rather distracting. You need to make a rule and stick to it: No listening to pop music while your son is doing homework. Only after his homework is completed and checked by a parent can he turn on "his" tunes. Show him the homework paper and explain that if he had read it carefully, he would have found the error himself. Point out that if he hadn't been listening to pop music, he wouldn't have written the wrong thing in the first place and probably would have finished more quickly.

Make sure your child has a quiet place to do homework and that he works at a desk or table, not on a bed. "Quiet" means no television, no music, no other family members around, and no telephone usage—in other words, no distractions. Emphasize to everyone in the household that homework time means quiet time so the student can concentrate and do his best.

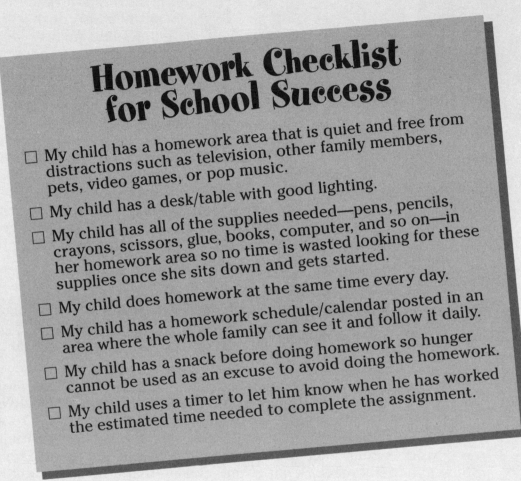

Homework Checklist for School Success

☐ My child has a homework area that is quiet and free from distractions such as television, other family members, pets, video games, or pop music.

☐ My child has a desk/table with good lighting.

☐ My child has all of the supplies needed—pens, pencils, crayons, scissors, glue, books, computer, and so on—in her homework area so no time is wasted looking for these supplies once she sits down and gets started.

☐ My child does homework at the same time every day.

☐ My child has a homework schedule/calendar posted in an area where the whole family can see it and follow it daily.

☐ My child has a snack before doing homework so hunger cannot be used as an excuse to avoid doing the homework.

☐ My child uses a timer to let him know when he has worked the estimated time needed to complete the assignment.

Snapshot #12:
My Child Says She Has No Homework

> **Remember: When the child, teacher, and parent are on the same team, success is inevitable.**

I ran into a friend of mine at the local supermarket whose daughter is in the same grade but a different class at my daughter's school. When she saw my daughter with me, my friend asked why she wasn't at home doing homework like her daughter was. When I looked at my daughter, she said simply, "I don't have any homework." I got to thinking, wondering why my friend's child had homework while mine always has so much free time. I found the school's parent handbook, which states the homework policy: "Homework is to be given daily." Either the teacher didn't follow the policy or my child was not doing the work. I began to get angry, thinking that my daughter wasn't learning as much as my friend's daughter. What should I do?

Tip: You need to contact the teacher to verify your child's statement. Call the school or write a note to ask for clarification of the teacher's homework policy. If you have the teacher's e-mail address, try contacting her that way; this may be the fastest way to get a response. Keep track of your communications. (See the following Homework Communications Tracking Sheet—Parent to School.) Share the supermarket conversation with the teacher and then ask about her homework policy. Tell her you check the planner/journal but many times nothing is written under "assignments." If she says she does assign homework nightly, then you need to talk to your child. Make it clear how important you feel school and homework are and that it is her job to complete her homework each night. Come up with a plan to improve your child's organizational skills and make sure she knows what is expected of her. Explain the consequences both at home and at school if things do not change. Suggest that you keep a chart or a spot in the planner/journal where (1) the teacher can initial that she received the completed homework, (2) you can note that you reviewed the work, and (3) your child can sign off that she completed her assignments as accurately as possible. (See the following Homework Team Completion Sheet.)

If during your conversation with the teacher she states she doesn't believe in homework, ask why and then dialogue to reach an understanding of her policies even though they differ from what is stated in the parent handbook. If you disagree, let her know that you feel homework is a time for home learning. Ask for resources so you and your daughter can practice skills at home. If you feel that the teacher is not providing enough time for skills acquisition and your child is not advancing enough, you may want to seek out other school personnel for guidance.

Sample Homework Communications
Tracking Sheet–Parent to School

Date/Form of Communication (Telephone, Note, E-mail)	Reason for Communication	Teacher Response	Date/Follow-Up Communication
1/10/06/ Note in planner	Child attempted math work but the two-digit multiplication was difficult.	Will work in small groups today.	1/12/06/Child seems to be catching on.

Sample Homework Team Completion Sheet

Date/Homework Assignment	Teacher's Signature	Parent's Signature	Child's Signature

2/1 4/ 06/ Math: Do pp. 10 #1-10.

    Write spelling words
for the week in
alphabetical order.

    Current events.

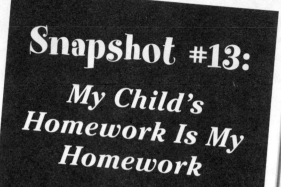

Snapshot #13:

My Child's Homework Is My Homework

I am spending too much time with my child on homework. I thought homework was simply a review of the day's schoolwork and should take a reasonable amount of time to complete. Many times it seems to be busywork; other times I get the feeling the necessary skills were not taught in class and the teacher expects me to do it. I don't always remember how to find the median number or when Lincoln was president or what blue and yellow make when they are mixed together. I am starting to suffer from homework anxiety. What should I do?

Tip : Fill in the Homework Communications Tracking Sheet (see Snapshot #12), then contact the teacher and ask for an immediate conference. (See the following sample letters.) Don't let the problem go too long; this is a serious situation the teacher needs to address immediately to help you and your child. The teacher should show you her homework policy and a typical day's work. Ask if your child is taking home class work she hasn't finished in school, whether she is grasping all concepts and skills taught, whether the homework focuses on new skills or reviews concepts taught in class. Continue to ask your child and yourself the following questions:

- Does my child comprehend the work?
- Is she staying focused in class?
- Is she as well prepared as she could be for school?

Once these questions are answered, then you, your child, and the teacher can work on solutions as a team. Reporting to each other on whether the solutions are working will keep stress levels down for everyone. You may want to use the Homework Checklist for School Success (see again Snapshot #11) and the following sample Monthly Homework-at-a-Glance Calendar to keep your child on track.

www.school-talk.com

Homework should not be an all-night project and it should be your child's work.

At conference time, ask:

1. How much time is a reasonable amount for my child to spend on homework?
2. Does unfinished class work become homework?
3. Is there homework assigned every night, including weekends?
4. How often are book reports assigned?
5. How often are science and/or social studies projects and reports given?
6. How much should a parent get involved?
7. How best can I help my child?
8. Are there any Web sites or software programs you can recommend to assist my child?

More Tips:

1. Remember, homework is the child's work.
2. A parent's role is that of adviser and checker.
3. Write a note or e-mail, or phone the teacher if your child doesn't understand a concept.
4. Praise your child's effort and good work.
5. If your child says his homework was done in school or in the afterschool program, check it and review it with him.
6. If your child says she has no homework and this goes on for several days, contact the teacher. Don't assume the child is always telling the truth.

Sample Letters for a Parent Requesting a Conference

Homework Is Too Difficult

Date:

Dear [teacher's name]:

I would like to request a meeting as soon as possible to discuss your homework policy. It seems like my son/daughter, [child's name], *is getting too much homework and has no time to relax when he/she gets home.*

Please contact me at _____ *anytime between 9:00* A.M. *and 5:00* P.M.

Thank you.

Sincerely,

[parent signature and printed name]

Homework Is Too Easy

Date:

Dear [teacher's name]:

I would like to have a conference with you as soon as possible to clarify your homework policy. My child, [child's name], *finishes his/her homework very quickly each night and I am wondering why it is so easy. Please give me a call at any time on my cell phone. My number is:* _____.

Thank you.

Sincerely,

[parent signature and printed name]

Not Enough or No Homework

Date:

Dear [teacher's name]:

Can we please set up a conference as soon as possible to review your homework policy? At this time, my child, [child's name], *comes home with very little homework or none at all. I would like my child to practice skills every night. I would appreciate your calling me on my cell phone* [number] *at any time during the day.*

Thank you very much.

Sincerely,

[parent signature and printed name]

Monthly Homework-at-a-Glance Calendar: Example #1

Month: _____

Monday	Tuesday	Wednesday	Thursday	Friday	Weekend
Spelling Math Writing	Spelling Grammar Start on project—visit library.	Math Language arts Buy materials for project.	Review spelling and math.	Start gathering information for project.	Start index cards for project and write first draft of report. Review rubric (details of what's expected) to make sure all information is on hand.
Spelling Math Writing	Spelling Grammar Continue writing the report draft.	Math Language arts Finish the report draft.	Review spelling and math. Edit the report draft.	Check spelling and grammar for the report.	Put the report into final form and add any pictures.
Spelling Math Writing	Spelling Grammar Start the model for the project.	Math Language arts Continue on the model.	Review spelling and math. Review for science test. Continue working on the model.	Finish the model.	Make a plan for getting the model to school on Monday.
Spelling Math Writing	Spelling Grammar	Math Language arts	Review spelling and math. Review for math quiz.	Read book for pleasure.	No homework

*Read nightly for a minimum of fifteen minutes.

Snapshot #14:

Turn in That Homework!

I am extremely disappointed with the grades my son received on his latest report card. What upsets me the most is that he failed to turn in some assignments, which contributed to his poor grades. While he is on grade level and not failing, his effort is below par and he doesn't seem to care. My dream is for him to attend college, but if he continues on this track of poor performance and indifferent attitude, I am worried this may not happen. What should I do?

> *Your vision may not be your child's. Work together and share dreams.*

Tip : The role of a parent should be to guide and advise her child throughout the school years, not to push. With your guidance and a continual dialogue, your child may reach his full potential. Set goals that are challenging yet realistic; do not expect him to achieve a level that may not be attainable. Handing in assignments, however, is definitely an achievable goal, and not doing so is inexcusable. Make a point to remind your child to hand in all assignments and help him work out a way to remember on his own. Keep in mind that when you emphasize the importance of excelling in school, a child will be motivated to meet your expectations. Remember to reward all efforts and set a good example. Continue your focus on education and your child's well-being. The grades and effort should follow.

One way to help your child remember his homework is to buy a folder and label it "Homework." Each night before school, you and your child can check the folder together to make sure all necessary papers are inserted and ready to hand in. With an older child, you can simply remind him, "Do you have your homework in your folder?"

Have your child put completed homework assignments in an "Inbox." This can even be a cardboard shoebox that your child may want to decorate. After you review the work and it's acceptable, place it in an "Outbox." That means your child can put it in her folder, which she then places in her backpack. If you find errors she needs to correct or if the work is not neat, point out what she needs to fix, have her make the changes, and then she can place it in the folder for school the next day.

Snapshot #15:

Long Division Is a Struggle for the Entire Family

My child's homework included a worksheet using a new way to do long division. He didn't understand it, my husband and I were confused, and when we asked my older son for help, he looked at the sheet as if it were written in a foreign language. No one in the house could give my younger son any help, which frustrated him, as he is not the type of child to hand in an incomplete paper. A horrible, stressful scene occurred, which distressed all of us. What should I do?

Tip : Have your child call a classmate and ask if he can explain the new skills and techniques to your child or to you. Your child should have a few telephone numbers of peers just for this purpose. You may want to keep this list handy, perhaps near the telephone or on the refrigerator. If you're still not able to figure out how to do the homework, write the teacher a note at the top of the homework sheet, giving a brief explanation. You might also try e-mailing the teacher. In the meantime, have your child do the steps he can do and reward him for trying. You don't want to say anything critical, such as, "Why don't you know this? Why weren't you paying attention?" Instead of using negative words, which only will heat up the situation, be positive. Try saying something like, "Boy, you know how to start and it looks like the first step is easy for you."

Reward a child both early and often. Delayed positive responses may delay success.

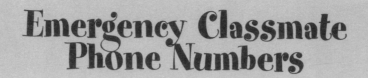

Emergency Classmate Phone Numbers

Friend #1 name: House phone:

Friend #2 name: House phone:

Friend #3 name: House phone:

Teacher's e-mail address:

School's phone number:

www.School-talk.com

Snapshot #16:
My Child Is Failing Homework and Schoolwork

My child is just not catching on to the skills being taught at school. Because she doesn't understand her schoolwork, homework is a complete waste of time. All assignments seem to be overwhelming and frustrating before she even opens up the books. Even writing down the assignments is a chore for her. When she sees how much work there is, she decides she just can't do it and will not even try. Every night we battle it out and usually she wins. What should I do?

> *Don't keep the steps too easy. Challenges are needed to encourage a sense of achievement.*

Homework Rewards Checklist

With your child, choose the number of points your child must earn to reach the reward. Make the goal attainable. Most children can work toward a weekly goal, while some children may need to get a reward nightly. Note what the reward will be. You may choose to take a child to a movie, out to eat, or to a special park, or to spend time just you two and no siblings—anything that shows how proud you are of her accomplishments.

Start with any three positive criteria goals listed as follows, or use your own. As your child completes each goal, award her FIVE points on the chart. Award a bonus of FIVE points when your child puts in an extra-special effort without any reminders from you. When your child fails to complete the goal, deduct FIVE points from the total score earned.

Tip : Ask for a conference with the teacher and school personnel immediately. Seek out their advice and assistance. Skill development is sequential, which means one skill builds upon another. Your child's teacher should be willing to help put together a plan so that your daughter is able to learn the necessary skills. As a parent and your child's first and foremost teacher, you must take pride in every accomplishment and encourage each small step in the process of learning. Think back to when your daughter was a toddler, learning to walk. You encouraged each baby step with clapping and cheering. That was a learning process, as is this. When you and the school have agreed on a plan to get your daughter up to speed, try turning homework into a game and offering rewards; this will build her self-confidence.

Continue to monitor your child's progress with the school team. If she still doesn't make any gains and her frustration at learning and doing homework continues, the team may suggest other strategies.

Homework Rewards Checklist

Point goal: _____   By what date: _____   Reward: _____

Points Earned Positive Criteria

____ Organizing your homework/study area

____ Starting homework/studying at designated time: _____

____ Keeping your room uncluttered

____ Putting all homework in your backpack for the next school day

____ Reviewing class notes

____ Completing all homework carefully and accurately

____ Giving Mom or Dad all school notes

____ Maintaining your positive attitude

____ Being cooperative

____ Completing all homework and studying without being reminded

____ Doing your best

Additional Positive Points for Extra-Special Efforts

Points Earned Positive Criteria

____ Reaching your studying goals

____ Completing assignments ahead of time

____ Receiving better test scores

____ Doing "extra credit"

____ Striving to become an Honor Roll student

Lost Points for Eliminating an Important Step

Points Lost Negative Criteria

____ Forgetting to hand in an assignment when it was due

____ Omitting a homework assignment

____ Neglecting to study a little each night

____ Ignoring the homework/study schedule

____ Not asking for guidance

____ Disregarding neatness and accuracy

Date: _____   Scores: + _____ − _____ = Total: _____

Snapshot #17:

How Do I Set Realistic Goals for School Success?

Make all goals specific and relevant.

My child had a disappointing semester this first quarter of school. Now that vacation is here, I would like to use the time to initiate a turnaround; otherwise, I'm afraid he may fail and be retained. He, too, has shown signs of being unhappy with his performance, as has the rest of the family, but we don't know how to proceed. What should I do?

Tip : You need to sit down with the family and create a road map for good grades. What do you want to see? How are you going to achieve this? Choose five realistic goals and have your child write them down. If he needs help, you can write them in his own words for him and then let him copy them. You might also want to write them on the computer and save them in a printed document as well. Some of the goals should be short term and some long term. For example, short-term goals may be to complete homework every night without assistance or to copy the homework from the board without disturbing classmates; a long-term goal could be to finish the year with all B's and C's or to graduate and go on to college. Put the goals on an index card and tape them to your child's bedroom door so he and the family can view them daily. As a goal is met, cross it out and jot down a new one, always keeping the number of goals at five. This provides visual motivation. At the end of each quarter, make a new list, keeping the goals not yet met as part of the new list. The role of family members is to motivate, support, and remind. The child's role is to keep focused, practice, and ask for help when needed. Accomplishing the short-term goals will make the long-term goals seem possible.

Get Onboard the Homework Success Train

Parent Involvement:

- Read nightly with your child even if it is not part of a homework assignment.
- Assist in projects (take your child to the library, buy the materials, give advice), but do not do work on the project.
- Know your child's learning style. Ask yourself whether he learns better if he:
  - Repeats facts to you.
  - Listens to tapes and memorizes the words.
  - Writes the key words several times, then repeats the facts.
  - Works with his hands, either feeling the letters or building three-dimensional figures.
- Ask specific questions about school and homework assignments.
- Check homework nightly to see that it is completed and done correctly. If it is not, see if you can help.
- Post a homework calendar—such as the Monthly Homework-at-a-Glance Calendar—in a spot where the entire family can see it. This is extremely helpful in viewing the homework schedule for the month.
- Celebrate the homework successes more frequently than you point out the failures.
- Give praise for the small steps. Don't always wait for the finished product. This assists in building self-confidence.
- Give consequences when your child is not doing his homework; this helps build responsibility.
- Discuss homework as a family.
- Provide your child with the opportunity to use homework skills in real-life situations. For example, you can practice math strategies at the supermarket by having the child use coupons, pay for the groceries, and receive the change. Other activities include having him budget his own allowance and learn measurements by cooking with you.

> *If you show that homework is important, your child will catch that feeling.*

Student's Role Checklist

It may be helpful to you as a parent to have your child complete the following checklists. It often helps to understand how your child views himself before starting a dialogue. These questionnaires will assist you in coming up with suggestions and give you and your child much-needed insight. The conversation with your child just might go more smoothly.

Student Assessment of Work Habits

Put a check in the box if you demonstrate these skills and attitudes, which will lead you to success in your schoolwork and on tests.

To Succeed, Do You:

☐ Work well with fellow classmates?

☐ Maintain clear focus on the teacher's lessons?

☐ Take pride in completed assignments?

☐ Pick challenging material for projects?

☐ Enjoy doing additional work over and above what the teacher assigns?

☐ Work well on your own?

☐ Rely on your own decisions, not your peers' ideas?

☐ Always try to do your best work and complete all tasks?

☐ Complete a draft or rough copy, edit, and then polish the final version?

☐ Demonstrate organizational skills?

☐ Forge ahead and review lessons nightly?

☐ Ask for assistance in a timely fashion when the assignment and/or concept is not understood?

Put a check in the box that best describes your current work and school behaviors.

If You Continue to Receive Poor Grades, Are You:

☐ Hurrying through class assignments and homework?

☐ Working better during structured lessons than in small groups?

☐ Handing in assignments without checking work, just to hand something in?

☐ Having to ask the teacher to repeat instructions and give additional information?

☐ Avoiding taking on responsibility during group assignments?

☐ Needing many reminders to stay on task?

☐ Bothering others around you continually?

☐ Performing better when work is put into smaller segments and given praise after each piece is explained?

☐ Copying work from other students and directly from books or the Internet?

☐ Receiving frequent late passes and/or unexcused absences?

☐ A follower, not a leader?

☐ Constantly striving to be the class clown?

☐ Often reprimanded by a teacher for not following class rules?

Snapshot #18:
My Child's Teacher Says He Needs a Tutor

M y child is just not doing well in school. While he's not failing, it takes him a long time to learn concepts and to finish his homework. I met with the teacher and she suggested some afterschool help. Every time I try to sit with my child to review and go over lessons, he fights me and develops a poor attitude. Obviously, I cannot be his tutor. The teacher feels that another adult may make the difference. I have no idea how to go about finding the right tutor. What should I do?

Tip : Take the time to investigate. Make phone calls to the guidance counselor, talk to parents whose opinion you respect, and ask the teacher if she knows of anyone. Interview the prospective tutor over the phone and then meet with her. Your ideal tutor will make learning fun, motivate your child to want to learn, and be knowledgeable in the subject area. Ask:

- What are your credentials?
- How long have you been a tutor?
- Do you have parents and students who would recommend you or references I may call?
- How will you assess my child for his strengths and weaknesses? How often will you assess?
- What programs will you use? (Get names and then check with the teacher.)
- Will you be in contact with my child's teacher so you both know what the other is doing to assist him?
- How long will each lesson be and how much do you charge?
- Do you allow a trial lesson at no charge to see if my child likes attending?

> *Finding the right tutor is just like buying a new piece of furniture. It may take some time, but it will be worth it to fine the perfect match. Once your child starts with the tutor, meet or stay in communication with the teacher to see whether progress is being made.*

Snapshot #19:

I Missed the Open House

Tip : Call the school and ask the teachers for a team meeting. If this won't work, ask other school personnel for the teachers' e-mail addresses. You can also check the school's Web site, where school events are often posted, as well as general information and important documents such as behavior codes and homework policies.

M y child never gave me the school flyer with details on the middle school open house. Since I do not drive my child to school, I never saw the notice on the school's marquee and I never thought to look on the school's Web site. I didn't find out about it until a friend called to tell me how glad she was that she had attended it. I now feel that I am at a disadvantage and so is my son, since I never found out the school policies or met the teachers. What should I do?

Attending major school functions lets your child know you consider education to be an important concern.

www.School-talk.com

What Should You Expect from Teachers and Schools?

If you can't answer yes to the following questions, you should ask the teacher or school administration to clarify the homework policy.

Does Your Child's Teacher:

- Give clear specific assignments?
- Inform parents of homework policies: How often, how much, weekends, projects?
- Explain guidelines for the weight given to homework completion in determining a student's grade?
- Provide tools, guidelines, or rubrics (detailing what's expected) to analyze each student's accomplishments on particular projects?
- Change strategies to become more effective if several students do not understand the day's lessons?
- Demonstrate what an exemplary project looks like before assigning one?
- Assign homework that reinforces lessons?
- Target skills that need to be practiced?
- Provide activities for students to demonstrate skills learned?
- Teach students to meet deadlines and take on responsibilities?
- Increase the home-school connection by asking parents to get involved on certain homework assignments?
- Make accommodations for homework for the special needs and LEP (Limited English Proficient) students?

Does Your Child's School:

- Have a schoolwide homework policy and inform parents of this policy?
- Collaborate with staff on developing homework procedures and guidelines?
- Keep up with the latest research on homework and inform parents of any new breakthroughs or changes?
- Send staff to professional development workshops to learn new ways to motivate students and parents?

Snapshot #20:

The Teacher Asks for a Resubmission

My daughter brought home a paper that had so many corrections it looked like the teacher thought she did everything wrong. I know my daughter worked many hours on this paper and even asked me to look it over. The work seemed fine to me and the cover was certainly appealing to the eye. I don't know what else she could have done and now the teacher wants a redo by tomorrow. What should I do?.

Respect the teacher who takes the time to write comments rather than just put a grade on the paper. Review the comments and encourage your child to learn from them.

Tip : You may want to sit down with your daughter and look over all the teacher's comments. There is a reason she wants a resubmission. There are probably key points your child didn't answer that were part of the assignment. The teacher took a lot of time to read all her students' papers and was careful to make suggestions and remarks. Your child had certain criteria to meet, and rather than giving her a failing grade for not doing so, the teacher is giving her another chance.

You may be upset now, but in the long run having a resubmit will teach your child to follow directions and listen more carefully. If there is a rubric or evaluation tool to follow, your daughter needs to learn how to look at that and meet all criteria before saying, "I'm finished." Editing is a valuable lifelong skill.

Snapshot #21:

The Dog Really Ate My Homework

Be Prepared Each and Every Day

Post a checklist in the kitchen or on the bathroom door or anywhere your child will spot it every day.

Your job is to remind him to check the list; his job is to read it and to get all the items ready all by himself.

The goal is to make getting ready for school an automatic part of the day without your child needing any reminders.

Preparedness Checklist:

____ Homework in folder
____ All textbooks in backpack
____ Lunch money or lunch in backpack
____ Pencils sharpened and in zippered compartment
____ Planner/journal in backpack
____ Extra notebook or loose-leaf paper in folder
____ School supplies in zippered compartment
____ Other (a note to the teacher, a school library book that's due, an instrument needed for band or music class, tennis shoes for PE, and so on)

My pet dog actually tore up my child's homework right before we got in the car to drive to the car pool. There was no time for me to write a note to the teacher or for my child to replace the assignment. We did try to tape it back together, but it was a poor attempt. My child was upset and I was so rushed to get the kids to school on time, I just couldn't deal with it right then. What should I do?

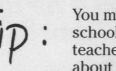

Tip : You may wish to call the school to give the teacher a heads up about why your child was so upset and that the dog really did attack the assignment; a teacher should be understanding and let a child redo the work sometime during the day or at home later that night. If your child has had this type of excuse before, the teacher may not be so understanding and instead ask to meet with you. In either case, you should come up with a plan so this doesn't happen again. You may want to make sure all important school papers are placed in your child's backpack the night before, which also gives you the opportunity to see what papers and information came home that day in the backpack. This way the entire family is more relaxed in the morning and may even have time for a family breakfast.

> *Have everything ready for school the next day, before your child goes to bed.*

Snapshot #22:

My Child Has Too Many Projects Due the Same Day

My son came home from school with a science fair project and a notice about an important quarterly exam on the same day that the project is due. Another teacher scheduled a major book report due a week later. I want my son to do his best, but this is asking too much. He needs to have some leisure time or I am afraid he will have a nervous breakdown. I think this time I have a right to complain. This is not fair to my son or any student. What should I do?

> *Students need to learn how to cope with occasionally heavy workloads. It gives them an insight into the challenges they'll face later on in "real life," as well as the tools to handle those responsibilities.*

Tip : This is a very important concept to teach your child. Students will always have multiple projects to prepare for. It is important to learn how to deal with these situations. Keep a monthly calendar or a weekly calendar (see the following examples) that you can view at a glance to see when major assignments and exams will be coming up. To facilitate success and organizational skills, help your child break down his school responsibilities into segments. Generally, teachers give enough advance notice for key exams and reports and often remind students of important dates. If you've tried helping your child break up the assignments into manageable chunks but he still can't handle the workload, then it is time to have a conference with his teacher.

Monthly Homework-at-a-Glance Calendar: Example #2

Month: _____

Monday	Tuesday	Wednesday	Thursday	Friday	Saturday	Sunday
6:30 Homework 8:30–9:00 Read*	4:30 Homework 7:00 Soccer practice 8:30 Read	4:30 Go to library for book for social studies report. 6:30 Homework 8:30 Study	4:30 Make outline for social studies report. 6:30 Homework 8:30 Make flash cards for studying.	4:30 Start to write down information for social studies report. 6:30 Homework 8:30 Study	7:00 Check rubric so I know that I have gathered all the information for social studies report. 8:30 Study	6:30 Review class work, pick a subject, and practice for a half hour even though no homework on weekends. Study notes for exam.
4:30 Write the first draft of the social studies report. 6:30 Homework 8:30 Study a little each night for Thursday's math test.	4:30 Edit the social studies report; do homework. 7:00 Soccer 8:30 Read	4:30 Have a parent read the social studies report for errors. 6:30 Homework 8:30 Read	4:30 Ask "Do I have the components to get an A on the social studies report?" 6:30 Homework 8:30 Read	4:30 Finish writing the social studies report. 6:30 Homework 8:30 Read	4:30 Do any artwork for the social studies report. 8:30 Read	6:30 Same as above.
4:30 Go to library for book for the book report. 6:30 Homework 8:30 Read the book for the book report.	4:30 Do homework and reading before soccer. 7:00 Soccer 8:30 Study	4:30 Give social studies report final review, put in backpack. Start on main characters from book in character trait chart, above, for the book report. 6:30 Homework Final review for Thursday's test. 8:30 Read	4:30 Fill in two boxes on character trait chart for the book report. 6:30 Homework 8:30 Read	4:30 Continue the chart. 6:30 Homework 8:30 Read	4:30 Finish the chart for the book report. 8:30 Read	6:30 Same as above. 6:30 Homework 8:30–9:00 Read
4:30 Homework 7:00 Soccer practice 8:30 Read	6:30 Homework 8:30 Read	4:30 Study Prepare for oral presentation on book report. 6:30 Homework 8:30 Read Make flash cards for oral presentation.	6:30 Homework 8:30 Read Study	8:30 Read Study	6:30 Review class work, pick a subject, and practice for a half hour even though no homework on weekends.	

*Read nightly for a minimum of fifteen minutes.

Weekly Homework Calendar Worksheet

Time	Monday	Tuesday	Wednesday	Thursday	Friday	Saturday	Sunday
4:30							
5:30							
6:00							
6:30							
7:00							
7:30							
8:00							
8:30							

Snapshot #23:

My Child Puts Great Effort into Homework Assignments, But That Is Not Enough

My child does everything she is supposed to when it comes to doing her homework. She goes to her designated spot, has a snack first, gets her books ready, and takes out her planner/journal. I never have to remind her. She's doing great, especially in comparison to what my friends go through with their kids, having to wage the nightly homework battle. The only problem I see is that she gets stuck on certain math problems and I just can't get her motivated to continue on.

What should I do?

www.school-talk.com

Tip : Talk to your daughter and ask her what exactly the problem is. Ask if she called a friend to assist and if she reread any class notes or the textbook to try to understand the concept. If she answers yes to all of these, then you may want to approach the teacher. Ask whether your daughter is focusing on the lessons and how she has tried to remedy the problem when she notices she just isn't catching on. You may want to ask your child whether she is giving up at the first signs of difficulty and then steer her to ask for help and to persevere.

> *Not everyone catches on the first time; learning takes practice and encouragement.*

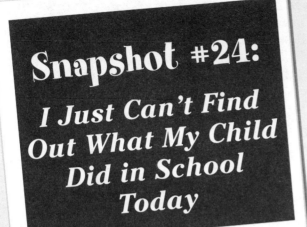

Snapshot #24:

I Just Can't Find Out What My Child Did in School Today

I know as a parent I am not supposed to get involved directly with my child's homework. I understand that he has to learn to be independent and that it's my job to promote learning and confidence-building activities. However, I feel that if I knew more about his class work I'd be better able to help him with his homework. When I ask my child what he is doing, the only answer I get is a grunt. I am frustrated at not knowing what's going on in his class and worried about his progress. What should I do?

Ask Guiding Questions:

- Ask about a math problem: "Which steps did you find easy or difficult?"
- Inquire about an oral presentation: "What parts did your friends like the best? Why do you think they liked it? What part did the teacher comment on?"
- Talk about the new story he read: "Was the character doing something you like to do? What was that? What qualities did the character have that would make you want to be his friend or get to know him better? Do you think I would like this story? Why or why not?"
- Ask what he learned about in social studies: "Did you know that when I went to school I loved to learn about the presidents just like you are learning now? My favorite was FDR because he was in office the longest. What facts did you read about?"
- Talk about his playtime: "I bet something exciting happened at recess. I would love to hear about it since my lunchtime was dull."

Tip : Asking your child "What did you do in school today?" and receiving the uninformative "Nothing" response can be frustrating, especially since you know he did lots of exciting things and learned something new. Perhaps the way you question your child or the type of question you ask is the reason. If your questions require only a yes or no answer, your child just might not be interested in answering. But if you ask thoughtful questions and show great interest, his response may be a little more informative. Add specifics to your questions, such as inquiring about a friend or a certain project or what game hc played at recess. Or start by telling him something about your day, and then bring the conversation back to what his day was like. Another possibility to consider is the tone of voice you use. You may be tired at the end of the day, but if you want to start a meaningful conversation, don't let it show in your questions. Change the pitch of your voice, become animated and excited. You just might get a long, detailed reply about what actually did happen in school.

Your Homework Assignment: The Homework State of Mind

Directions: Now that you have completed Chapter Two, take some time to answer the following questions. This is a short assignment that will act as a review and, we hope, increase your understanding of the key points.

1. What is your role in helping your child avoid homework tension?

2. List three things you can do to encourage your child to become "homework-savvy."

    a.

    b.

    c.

3. How do you organize your child's homework space at home?

CHAPTER THREE
No More Homework Hassles

> "What I hear, I forget. What I see, I remember. What I do, I understand."
> **Confucius**

Now that you have the knowledge to create an optimal learning environment, how can you apply that to your own child's situation? This chapter gives you the edge you need when dealing with the reality of homework. Some examples:

- Is your child the star soccer player but never seems to have time for homework?
- Does your child have the homework blues?
- Does your child take hours to do homework?
- Is your child's teacher giving homework that does not follow the daily lesson?
- Is your child receiving poor grades?

This chapter provides handy checklists, along with worksheets, suggestions, and tips you can use to organize homework responsibilities. Snapshots once again clearly explain the role of the parent, the child, and the school. The practical advice shows you how to turn negative situations into positive ones. The "homework assignment" at the end of the chapter will help you reflect on the information presented and assist in getting rid of the nightly battle over homework.

You're on your way to no more homework hassles!

www.school-talk.com

Snapshot #25:

My Child Doesn't Understand How to Do His Homework

My son gets an awful lot of homework every night, and it's causing a disruption in our family life. I get home from work, tired myself, with very little time to get dinner and do a few chores. Then I hear him say, "Mom, I don't understand this reading question," and I just begin to panic. I have to drop everything to help him. Nothing will get done and we have to eat takeout food again if he's going to get to practice on time. That old saying, "So much to do, so little time," describes our hectic lifestyle. What should I do?

Balance your and your child's time.

A simple Weekly Homework Assignment Checklist will help your child become better organized and avoid wasting time. Your child may find that these extra minutes give him the time he needs to go outside, play with friends, practice his favorite instrument, and so on.

Tip : First, take a deep breath. Then consider some reorganization to regain balance for you and your child in the home, at school, and with outside activities. Ask yourself questions such as: Are we doing too much? Do we just need a better schedule to be put in place? Or do we need to drop some activity to find balance? Remember, when planning outside activities, make sure your child knows schoolwork comes first. Both you and your child need "downtime," and maintaining friends is important too. Devise a schedule together and let him know you expect him to follow it. (See the following example.)

69

Sample Weekly Homework Assignment Checklist

Before starting homework do I:

Have a quiet area to do my homework?	Yes	No
Know what homework needs to be done?	Yes	No
Have supplies needed to do my work successfully?	Yes	No

Day of the week: _____

Subject:	Homework Assignment	Completed
Math	Do pp. 14–15 (odd numbers)	
Reading	Read chapter 1 pp. 1–10	
Spelling	None	
Science	None	
Social studies	Answer questions 1–5 on pg 42	
Writing	None	
Grammar	None	
Art/music	None	
Other	Have Mom sign field trip permission form	

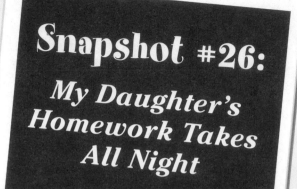

Snapshot #26:

My Daughter's Homework Takes All Night

Questions to think about and to ask the teacher:

- Does my child finish her class work? Are you assigning incomplete class work as homework?
- Does my child focus on the lesson being taught?
- How long do you expect a child to work on homework to complete it?
- How do you want me to help? Should I go over the assignments and point out the errors or should I just check for completion?
- Can we shorten the assignment load as long as my child gets the decreased amount entirely correct?
- Are the assignments an extension of school lessons or do they present new skills?

My daughter sticks to the homework schedule the family has put together. She has time to play when she gets home, followed by dinner with the family, and then it's immediately off to her desk to start her homework. She knows the rules: No distractions and do your best. Yet when it gets close to time to bathe and go to bed, her homework is incomplete. I look over the assignments and it doesn't seem to be an unfair amount. What should I do?

Tip: First, stop at bedtime! Sleep is vital. Second, find out why she cannot complete her work in a reasonable time. Call the teacher and ask for a conference immediately. It is essential to find out the problem and rectify it. Maybe as a team you can discover a way to assist your child through this homework dilemma.

www.school-talk.com

Snapshot #27:

My Child Doesn't Listen to Me When I Ask Her to Do Her Homework

Every day after school it is a battle from the minute we walk in the door. My daughter puts down her backpack wherever she wants, turns the TV on high volume, then gets on the phone for what seems to be hours. She just saw her friends in school; what could be so important that she has to speak to them again before starting her homework? I ask her to get started on the assignments, but invariably I have to remind her several times—usually at the top of my voice—before I can get her off the phone or away from the television and working on her homework. It is the same routine day in and out. What should I do?

Ask once and then follow through with consequences.

Tip : You shouldn't have to repeat yourself. Unfortunately, your daughter knows nothing will happen to her if she ignores you, so why should she do what you ask the first time? In this case, your daughter has control and all you have is frustration and anger.

Time to take control! Set limits for the telephone and TV and let her know what they are. Create a schedule for homework and decide what the consequences will be when you have to ask her more than once to do it.

Now comes the hard part—enforcing those consequences. No matter how old she is, she may throw a temper tantrum, slam doors, scream at you, and use harsh words, but you must stand firm. She has to learn that you mean business and that homework comes before TV and the telephone. Make sure all the adults in the household agree on this new policy and will enforce the new rules.

Snapshot #28:

My Child Is Not Motivated to Get Good Grades

My child is receiving C's and D's. No matter what I try to do, I can't get him motivated. He's happy just getting by from year to year. He does the minimum amount of homework and his research projects show very little effort. He has been tested and the doctors tell me that there is nothing wrong with him. They suggest a little shove in the right direction might get him to do more. I have tried to push him, but nothing seems to work. I just don't know what to do to turn this around. I want him to become productive and have dreams and goals. What should I do?

Says Dr. Norman Vincent Peale: "If there is no fun in it, something is wrong with all that you are doing."

See Appendix C, "Parent Involvement: Learning Fun Collection," for fun and educational activities you can do with your child.

Tip : Find out what really motivates your son, something fun he'd like to do. Then devise a system of realistic goals for him to reach and corresponding rewards. (See the contracts provided in Snapshot 29 in this chapter and in Snapshot 42 in Chapter Four.) Once he makes it to the final goal, keep your promise and reward him with the fun activity. Don't put it off! We all like getting rewarded as quickly as possible; otherwise, the promise of that reward loses its positive impact.

Some children may need an immediate reward for the little steps they take. For example, if he does half of the math problems correctly, you might give him some M&M's or popcorn. When he completes the other half, he can have the rest. Pick out the reward that works best and then be consistent in your implementation. Show your child that you care, and just maybe that care and concern will wear off on him.

Snapshot #29:

My Child Fails to Copy His Homework Assignments

A plan only works if you perform, perform, and perform it some more.

I am beginning to think my child is lazy—either that or he just doesn't understand how important homework is because it lets him practice what he has learned. I have spoken to him and so has his teacher about his role as a student. When the students come in each morning, the teacher has the homework assignment written on the board for them to copy. I make sure my son arrives early so he has extra time to write down the assignment. But the teacher says it takes him a long time to get organized each morning because he has to flit around and talk to everyone before he settles down. This cuts into his time for copying the assignment and keeps him from getting the day started on the right foot. What should I do?

Homework contracts are NOT made to be broken.

Tip: It's time to draw up a Student Homework Contract, which must be agreed to and signed by all team members. (See the following worksheet.) Arrange a meeting with your child and his teacher. Discuss what your child's homework responsibilities are, both in school and at home. Let him know that the adults' role will be to make sure he does his part. Decide on a program of rewards and consequences for both school and at home, then stick to it. Be consistent in rewarding him when he follows the contract and in handing out consequences when he does not. (For more on contracts, see Chapter Four.)

Sample Student Homework Contract

Date:

Child's signature: _____

Parent's signature: _____

Teacher's signature: _____

1. I will copy the homework from the board as soon as the teacher writes it.
2. I will bring home all the books necessary to complete the assignments.
3. I will start to do my homework at my scheduled time.
4. I will start and complete my homework without reminders from an adult.
5. I will ask for help when I need it.
6. I will have my parent look over my completed work.
7. I will be neat.
8. I will be organized.
9. I will get my friend's phone number so if I have questions or forgot something, I can call her for help.
10. I will remember to put the completed assignments in my backpack immediately so I do not forget to take them to school.

Snapshot #30:

The Coach Says Practice, Practice, Practice to Make the Basketball Team. I Say Do Homework, Homework, Homework to Make the Success Team

My son has come home with the wrong message—or maybe the right message, but in the wrong place. The coach has told him the only way he is going to be a starter on the basketball team is by practicing at least an hour every day. This daily practice cuts into my son's time for homework and his grades are starting to drop. My philosophy that practicing homework skills makes him a "winner" has been completely lost. I know sports are important, but so is schoolwork.

What should I do?

> **Sometimes too much free time becomes wasted time.**

Tip: Children who must juggle school with outside activities run into problems if they don't know how to use their time wisely. Taking away a fun activity, such as a sport, may not solve the problem; the child may end up wasting that newfound time rather than using it wisely. Creating and sticking to a schedule can help keep children on track and lead to success both in school and on the team.

Draw up a monthly homework calendar (see the sample Monthly Homework-at-a-Glance Calendars in Chapter Two). Sit down with your child and fill out the calendar together. Emphasize the importance of striking a balance between completing schoolwork and participating in an afterschool activity. Let him know that nothing can interfere with getting good grades, and if his grades fall, you will pull him off the team until they improve. Make it clear this is not negotiable. Also, let his coach know how you feel about schoolwork and the conditions under which your child may play on the team.

Snapshot #31:

I Don't Understand Why the Teacher Gives Such Elaborate Projects for Homework

Play is a form of learning.

My child's teacher is known as "The Project Queen." Simply assigning a report isn't enough; she also requires some kind of visual work, such as three-dimensional art. I never understood the purpose in assigning all these difficult projects. Having the students do a report should be enough. Too often the artwork seems like busywork. Judging by the finished products, these elaborate art projects are not the best use of my son's time and talents, and they take up time that could be used better another way. Not only does it take my child forever to do these projects, I have to spend time and money on the weekends to go out and buy the materials. What should I do?

Tip: Think back to when you were in school. If you're like most people, the assignments you remember best—and probably were your favorites—were those where you did something with your hands. Remember the science lesson in which you learned how to make a volcano erupt or the math lesson where you made a clock so you could learn how to tell time? You probably think about those lessons with a smile because you had fun while you were learning the new skills.

Making learning fun is only one of the reasons why a teacher assigns supporting projects for a report. Sometimes projects are difficult to do in school because of a lack of room, no sink in the classroom, not enough time to complete the entire process, and other limitations. Another good reason is that the teacher may want students' parents to become involved in the project process.

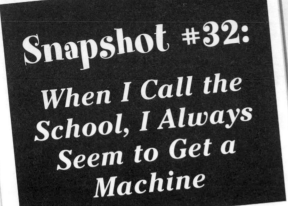

Snapshot #32:

When I Call the School, I Always Seem to Get a Machine

Give your child an educational advantage. Purchase a safe Internet connection. Check with an Internet access company to find out how you can block sites you do not want your child to view or have access to. Remember, you still need to look over his shoulder every once in a while to check on what he is viewing.

Try these sites free of charge:

www.scienceideas.org
www.starfall.com
www.funbrain.com

www.scholastic.com
www.edhelper.com

I have a hard time getting information from my son's school. My child doesn't bring home a school newsletter. Whenever I call the school, I don't get a live person but am directed to an automated voice mailbox. My son's teacher never returns my telephone calls. I feel I am not being informed about the school events or my son's progress in a timely manner and I can never talk to a real person to get some questions answered. Sometimes I feel his grades are suffering because of this lack of communication. I know technology is the new wave in education, but there are things I just don't want to put in writing via an e-mail, and talking to an actual person would be nice. What should I do?

There are educational Web sites and software that support school curricula. Ask the teacher for assistance.

Tip : Although the new technology may take a bit of getting used to, it actually puts more information at your fingertips. Homework is often posted on the teacher's Web site. School events, lunch menus, calendars, and even lesson plans are posted on the school's Web site. The teachers are available via e-mail. Lessons are being taught by PowerPoint presentations, and your child is more than likely taking a computer class at least once a week, works on computers in his classroom, and uses the Internet to look up information. Classrooms even have educational software that acts as a tutor to help improve students' skills.

To solve the problem of wanting to speak directly with the teacher, I would e-mail her and ask for a conference. Specify your available dates and times and give her all relevant telephone numbers: home, work, and cellular. If she doesn't respond, write a note or make time before or after class to see her to schedule the conference. If you try all of the communication tools that are at hand and you are still frustrated at the lack of response, plan to have a meeting with administration.

Snapshot #33:
My Child Has the Homework Blues

Every day after school, my child and I go through the same old routine. "I work hard all day long in school," she complains. "Why do I have to do more work at home? Besides, this is just busywork. I know this stuff already. I barely have time to do the things I want." I explain that homework lets her practice the skills taught in school and shows the teacher she understands the concepts so she can continue on to the next level. But she still finds some excuse to avoid doing it when she should, and the battle continues. Eventually the homework gets done, but it's never a smooth ride. Bribery sometimes works, but I know that's not the right way to go about it. I just want her to be a good student and love school. Am I asking too much? What should I do?

Tip: You are the child's first teacher and role model. Rather than argue with her, consider doing such activities as reading, writing, or searching the Internet while she is working

> **Be a role model and take a real interest.**

on her homework. Show enthusiasm while you do these activities. It is so important that you emphasize the positive, because children mirror what they see. She just might decide that if you enjoy it, so might she. If you shut the television off to read a book, your child will understand—without your reminders—that reading is fun and valuable. She'll be more inclined to turn off the television and open a book.

Another trick you may try is to show a greater interest in what she is working on. Ask questions. Look at the work and offer your praise and encouragement. Try to open a discussion about the homework. You may want to say something like "What was the story about?" "Why did that happen to the boy in the story?" "Can I read this with you?" For older children, you might ask what the science experiment proved, why it worked out the way it did, or whether there were any other methods that could produce the same results. In the end, taking these few minutes out of your day will make a difference, turning a child who uses every excuse not to get started and complete assignments into one who is motivated to do homework.

If this fails and the battles persist, you need to see the teacher and discuss your child's issues about the homework being too easy and boring. The instructor just may have answers for you. One idea for motivating your child is to let her pick out a topic she would like to give a report on. As long as the necessary skills are covered, she might find the motivation that is lacking.

Guide to Asking Questions When Reading with Your Child

If your child is reading a book for pleasure, you may want to ask:

- What is the story about?
- Who is your favorite character? Why?
- Where does the story take place and is it a place you would like to visit? Why?
- Why do you think the author wrote this story?
- If you could rewrite the ending, what would you write?
- Why do you think the author chose to tell this story?
- Would you recommend that I read this book? Why do you think I would like it?

If your child has to review a newspaper or magazine article, you may want to ask:

- What is the article about?
- In which part of the paper did you find it?
- Why was this article important?
- Do you think the article told you all the facts? If not, what more would you like to find out?
- Who was the article about?
- When and where did it take place?
- If you were the reporter, would you have told the story the same way? How could you have written it differently?
- Where can you find out more information about this story?

Snapshot #34:

My Child's Teacher Doesn't Communicate Homework Policies or Problems

I am never quite sure what the teacher's homework policy is. Does she give homework every night? Does the homework she gives review the skills taught in school? When I ask my child these questions I never get a straight answer. And although I check his backpack every day, sometimes he has homework, other times he does not. On a couple of occasions I've gotten a note days after it was due that my son needs to turn in his homework. Now I've received a note saying my child has missed several homework assignments and therefore his grades are falling. What should I do?

Remember, an effective conference will take place only if there is active listening and talking. The more we listen, the more we can learn from each other and then move in the direction of planning positive goals.

You may want to review the following Teacher Homework Survey with your child's teacher at a parent night or at a teacher conference to gain insights into the teacher's homework policies.

Tip : First, speak with your child about how the teacher gives out homework assignments and what her expectations are. If you cannot get a clear answer, tell your son you are going to call the teacher for a conference to find out what is going on in class. During your conversation, ask the teacher to clearly define her homework policy for you. You may want to ask her why she has taken so long to let you know about this problem and why she hasn't telephoned. If she has sent home an incomplete homework notice that you never saw, tell her you will take this up with your child. However, if she sends home another notice in the future, ask her to contact you so you can be on the lookout for it. You may want to come up with a homework policy where a parent has to sign the journal/planner (which can be made using a notebook or may be provided by the school; see Chapter Two) and the actual completed homework papers. Using a Communication Report Log like the following may help you keep track of all communications and outcomes.

81

Sample Communication Report Log

Date	Who Called for the Conference?	Who Was Present?	Why Was the Conference Called?	Outcome	Follow-Up Date
Oct. 9, 2006	Teacher	Teacher/parent	Not bringing in math homework	Parent will sign homework daily	Oct. 23, 2006

Teacher Homework Survey

1. What is the most important reason for assigning homework?
2. How much homework is a realistic amount?
3. How much does homework completion count in your grading system?
4. Do you let parents know your homework policies?
5. Do you make homework accommodations for special-needs students?
6. Are your homework assignments used as a supplement to your daily lessons?
7. Do you check your students' completed homework nightly and do you correct errors to provide feedback?
8. Do you look at the completed assignments and analyze who needs additional help?
9. Do you let parents know immediately when homework is not being done?
10. Are you incorporating parent involvement in your homework assignments, at least once a week?
11. At open house and/or parent night meetings, do you give parents and students advice on how to organize their homework/projects and how best to schedule them into their daily lives?
12. Do you vary your homework assignments? How?
13. In your opinion, which is more effective: daily assignments (with immediate feedback) or weekly homework packets, sent home on Monday and expected to be completed by Friday (students work at their own pace)? Why?
14. Do you give additional small-group instruction to the students who are struggling with homework skills?

Snapshot #35:

No One Listens to a Word I Say

> *Listen as though what your child has to say is the most important part of your day. Let your child know you will always make the time to listen.*

My child ignores my attempts to have a conversation. I feel like I am running into a brick wall. All I want is to have some dialogue about how things are going—school, friends, teacher, homework, and learning. Is that too much to ask? According to my daughter it is. She's too tired in the afternoons; in the morning, it's so hard to get her out of bed we're always rushed. I am lucky if a get a "Good morning" or "See you later." Most of our conversation centers around lunch money and where she will be after school. I know she is a teenager, but I find being shut out unacceptable. What should I do?

Tip : Be an active listener with your child. Engaging in a meaningful conversation is not just having something to say, but more importantly, letting the other person know you are listening and genuinely interested. Show her what she's saying is important to you by looking straight at her when she is talking and repeating the key words or phrases she says in your own responses. This is not an easy thing to do, but well worth the emphasis when dialoguing with your child. Remember to ask questions and have the conversation in an area free of distractions (other siblings, television, the telephone, and so on).

No matter how tired or rushed you are, make time for listening to your daughter. If you show a genuine interest and share your own thoughts, she will start to converse with you more. Don't put it off for a later time, because that time may never come.

Snapshot #36:

My Child Always Waits to the Last Minute to Complete His Work

It is inevitable. A couple of days before he has a project due, my child comes running into the house from school, yelling, "Mom, my project is due the day after tomorrow! We have to get to the store right now or I won't be able to hand it in on time!" He has worked himself into a panic and I'm annoyed at having to drop everything I'm doing and help him fix this problem. The stress level goes up for everyone, and it's just not fair to the rest of the family. When is he going to learn to plan out his work in a timely fashion? What should I do?

www.school-talk.com

Tip : A monthly schedule will help, but it may not be enough to teach your son how to become organized. Try using the following Project Day-by-Day To-Do List, which spells out exactly what tasks he should perform each day. The list offers a more comprehensive way to keep your child on track by having him work on projects a little each night. This approach ensures smoother and more structured evenings, reduces stress for everyone, and helps your child create a better-quality final project.

Project Day-by-Day To-Do List

Day 1: The day the assignment is given out by the teacher.

- Place due date on the monthly calendar.
- Outline your ideas.
- Share your ideas and the due date with your parents.
- Tell your parents what materials you will need and whether you need their assistance. Make a comprehensive list.
- Work out a plan that will help you manage the time needed for the project. Ask yourself how much time you will spend on the project each night until it is completed.

Day 2: Post the rubric by your desk so that you can refer to it as you move through the steps. (A rubric is a list detailing what is expected in a project or assignment.)

- Check off each item on the rubric as you complete it, doing your best work so you can receive the highest grade. Jot down any questions you might want to ask the teacher the next day in school.

Day 3: Plan the research.

- Do you need to go to the library?
- Do you bring home all the school books you need every night?
- Do you need to use the computer?

Day 4: Get work area ready.

- Put necessary books and supplies at your desk. Have a snack and make sure there will be no distractions.

Day 5: Look over the project and decide how to start.

- If it is a group project, speak with group members and divide up the responsibilities. Get everyone's phone and e-mail numbers.
- If it is a one-person project, divide the project into parts and then number all of them in the order you will complete them.

Day 6: Write a first draft, editing as you go, then reread.

- Edit information for accuracy the first time around.

Day 7: Complete second draft and edit.

- Check spelling, grammar, and information. Are the words spelled correctly? Are there any run-on sentences? Are your ideas clear and precise? Is all the information there to answer the rubric criteria?
- Is the draft neat and accurate?
- Is it in your own words? Remember, no direct copying.

Day 8: Work on any hands-on artwork (time lines, drawings, three-dimensional renditions, maps, and so on).

- Make sure everything is labeled and has a title.
- Is it neat and accurate?
- Did you answer everything on the rubric?

Day 9: Complete.

- Put together the final project, including the visual pieces and the research.
- Does it look like it deserves an A?

Day 10: Project due date.

- Bring the project in on time.

Parent's Role:

1. With your child, put the project due date on the calendar.
2. Be prepared to go shopping for any necessary supplies.
3. Remind but don't nag your child to do a little each night. It is his responsibility to get it completed. Do not make it your project or problem.
4. Check nightly on your child's progress. Applaud the effort.
5. Give ideas and suggestions, but do not do the project.
6. Be ready to go to the library for additional books and reference materials.
7. Review the draft before the final copy is done.
8. Call the teacher if your child is struggling with any part of the project.
9. Be ready to bring your child to school the day the project is due in case it is too big to carry on the school bus.
10. Reward your child for a job well done. Let him know you are proud that he did it on his own and the final product shows he worked hard on it. Smile and congratulate him.

Your Homework Assignment: No More Homework Hassles

Directions: Now that you have completed Chapter Three, take some time to answer the following questions. This is a short assignment that will act as a review and, we hope, increase your understanding of the key points.

1. How do you encourage and motivate your child to stick to a homework schedule?

2. List three questions about homework situations you could ask when conferencing with your child's teachers.

   a.

   b.

   c.

3. How often do you check the school's Web site?

4. What are the consequences if your child does not complete homework assignments?

5. How can you show your child that you believe that homework is very important?

CHAPTER FOUR
The Homework Contract

"The beginning is the most important part of the work."
Plato

Forgotten homework . . . Overdue projects . . . Reports left to the very last minute . . .

When outside assignments aren't completed in a timely manner, who is responsible?

Ultimately, the student must be responsible for his work, but parents play an important role in helping their child successfully fulfill that responsibility. As a parent, you are an integral part of the school success team, and one of your most important tasks is to promote strong homework habits.

Think about it. Do you want to be the parent who must hurriedly run out to buy materials, then stay up late to finish your child's science project, which is due the next day? Or would you rather work with your child at a steady pace over several days, guiding him toward finishing his project on time and without stress?

More important, which scenario is better for your child?

Homework requires commitment and responsibility, two important values to instill in our children. It also helps children succeed in school. For all of these reasons, homework should take priority in every child's life. Defining the individual roles of the student, teacher, and parent, along with creating a homework contract, will help your child develop good homework habits.

This chapter will address these issues. It will offer suggestions and guidelines on several kinds of homework contracts, so you can choose one best suited to your and your child's needs. It will:

- Clearly spell out who is responsible for what.
- Assist you in making a contract.

www.school-talk.com

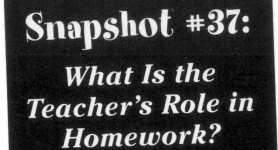

Snapshot #37:

What Is the Teacher's Role in Homework?

The Homework Planner/Journal

Teaching children good habits begins with organization. Does your child's teacher provide your child a homework log or journal where she can write the daily assignments? In this book, the child needs to write each and every assignment given by the teacher. By instilling this habit into your child's daily routine, she will learn to be much more responsible. Fewer homework assignments will be lost or forgotten, and a good habit will be formed when your child is using the daily journal. Be sure to make very specific rules about missing assignments. If the teacher is not providing this for your child you may want to purchase a calendar book, memo pad, or composition book to use as a substitute.

My daughter often comes home from school with assignments she doesn't understand. While I recognize that children don't always pay close enough attention to the teacher's instructions, I also want to make sure the teacher is providing my child with enough information. What should I do?

Tip: Believe it or not, the teacher plays a very important role in homework! The teacher needs to provide both oral and written instructions on how to do the assignments. Written instructions need to detail more than just the number of problems required—they should also include learning objectives, a sample answer, an approximate answer length, a list of ideas to be included in the answers, and acceptable resources. (For instance, is the student allowed to use the Internet? Is this a textbook-only project?) If the assignment counts for a large part of a grade or is a complex undertaking, the best teachers provide rubrics—or guidelines—on how the work will ultimately be evaluated.

But the teacher's role extends beyond giving adequate instructions. It is a teacher's job to motivate students to work on assignments by showing WHY this topic is helpful to the students on a personal level. Studies show that the most effective assignments are often "real-world" assignments that connect the subject matter to the student's life. The teacher's role in the homework process is also to provide useful and immediate feedback, which, if done well, increases academic achievement. And of course, the teacher is responsible for determining the amount of homework assigned. Although studies indicate that homework is beneficial, one accepted guideline is based on research gleaned from one hundred studies of homework. This research was compiled by Harris Cooper, a psychology professor at the University of Missouri. The guideline suggests ten to twenty minutes every night at first grade and then a ten-minute increase per each succeeding grade level.

Snapshot #38:

What Is the Parents' Role in Homework?

ast year, at the school science fair, several projects were exhibited that were clearly well beyond the ability of any elementary student I've ever known. Of course, I suspect the parents actually did the project and the child went along for the ride. Many of these projects received an A. I mentioned this to the teacher and asked what about the role of the parent. She was very vague and did not give me a direct answer. I really want my child to succeed on his own merit, but also want to help him. What should I do?

www.school-talk.com

Tip : Your experience at the science fair is not at all unique. I suspect that most parents have had similar suspicions. However, a parent should be a coach, not a player. First, parents should always be aware of the child's homework assignments. This allows them to share ways in which this knowledge is helpful in everyday life. They can mentor the child, provide additional insight, or suggest different approaches to thinking about a topic. Second, parents can make sure that a child fulfills the requirements of the assignment and that the child understands how to do the problems. Certain projects require the parents' help, such as recommending people to interview, or providing materials, or helping in the actual design of the project. But parents should not DO the assignment for the child.

It's human nature to want to look good and to want your child to be the best. However, if education is the real reason for assigning homework, it doesn't help anyone for parents to do the work. Even if your child's project doesn't look nearly as professional as the one his friend made—and whose engineer mother actually built it—praise and encourage him for his effort and make him proud of the fact that he did it HIMSELF. Part of learning is doing, and the child learns a lot more if he does it himself than if someone helps him too much.

The Do's and Don'ts of Homework

Do:

- If your child attends an afterschool program you may want to know if the afterschool program has a homework component; many afterschool programs provide a homework room with assistance for those children who need it.
- Set aside the same time each day for your child to do homework.
- Set up an area in your house that is quiet where your child can do homework.
- Turn off the TV.
- Play soft music, not pop music, in the background, if it's not too distracting—some children work better this way.

Do not:

- Let your child complete the homework at school (unless the teacher allows it).
- Let your child talk you into doing his assignments.
- Let your child tell you there are no assignments for two or more days in a row.
- Let your child say the homework is complete without you looking at it.

Snapshot #39:

What Is the Student's Role in Homework?

I am a newly graduated teacher who will be starting her first full-time teaching job next fall. I want to have a clearly developed list of expectations for my students. I want to provide parents with policies and guidelines that will clarify the child's role in completing homework. What should I do?

Children need to learn to be responsible for their own homework.

Tip : It's very helpful when policies and ideas are clearly spelled out for students, so I applaud your efforts. The student has five basic responsibilities when it comes to homework.

1. The student must keep a record of what kind of homework she has to do, either by copying down instructions from the board into a homework log or carrying home a list or instruction sheet developed by the teacher.

2. The student should ask questions about the assignment if she doesn't understand it. Teachers can encourage students' understanding by having a session at the end of the day that reviews assignments and asks whether anyone has questions or concerns.

3. The student is responsible for working on the assignment at home. If there are questions that can't be answered, the student should write a note on the sheet explaining why it isn't answered.

4. The student should talk to a parent about the homework. Parental involvement in assignments can sometimes clarify a problem or provide desperately needed encouragement.

5. The student is responsible for bringing the assignment back to school on the due date. Often—even very often—children leave work on the kitchen table, on their desk, in the car—anywhere but in their backpack ready for school the next day.

Snapshot #40:

My Child Doesn't Want Help with Her Homework

My eight-year-old daughter always tells me she wants me to leave her alone when she does her homework. I'd have no problem with that—in fact, I'm proud of her independent nature. However, I've noticed recently that she's getting a lot of things wrong on her work or not doing the assignment correctly. What should I do?

> **Open communication is one of the best "helps" a parent can give!**

Tip : Isn't it wonderful that your daughter already has that sense of self and independence? Most parents can help their children at home with just simple monitoring and sincere interest in what they are doing. You can offer a great amount of help by making sure your daughter has a quiet, spacious area to do homework. Another thing you can do is help her structure a homework routine. For instance, does she want to do homework immediately after school, or would it be beneficial if she had some time to wind down and burn off energy before she sits down and concentrates? If she wants help on an individual problem, then by all means, feel free to give her guidance, but respect your daughter's independence if she doesn't ask for help.

Some children don't want a parent hovering over them, checking each answer or assignment. You might try discussing your daughter's assignments with her before she does them. Use the opportunity to share your interest in what she's doing. Parents should also review the homework assignments after they've been completed, making suggestions or offering praise as needed. If your daughter has not followed the instructions exactly, or if she has gotten a lot of answers wrong, it's possible you can point this out after she finishes the assignment.

Snapshot #41:

I Never Expected to Spend So Much Time Monitoring My Child's Homework

Be proactive simply by knowing what concepts your child struggles with and by making recommendations on how to help your child deal with these struggles.

I sometimes get frustrated by the amount of time I spend monitoring my child's homework activities every night. Can you remind me why I'm doing this and reassure me that this is worth the effort? I am losing patience. What should I do?

Tip: Your frustration is understandable, particularly in this world where often both parents have a job in the workplace as well as household chores, like cooking, cleaning, doing laundry, and chauffeuring kids to a dozen different activities each week. Some evenings you might not feel like spending time being the "homework police" as well. But rest assured, your efforts are well worth it, because children benefit immensely from parents who are involved as mentors and guides in homework.

Your child might gain a new appreciation of your knowledge and insight. Learning becomes more real to a child who hears from a knowledgeable adult how this kind of information is important in the world outside of school. Children also benefit from being able to talk to a parent about all kinds of topics. Suddenly, it's more like having a conversation than being told what to do or taking directions, and your child may be able to "teach" you something. This interplay is not only beneficial to a child's self-esteem but also provides the motivation to learn more. An added benefit is that when a parent acts as a homework guide, any difficulties the child might have become apparent early on, giving you an opportunity to find solutions before they become real problems.

Snapshot #42:

I Need a Homework Contract. Where Can I Find One?

I've heard a lot about homework contracts. Can you tell me what they are and show me what kind of agreement I might have as a parent with my child? I really want to help my child succeed. What should I do?

www.school-talk.com

Tip : Homework contracts, quite simply, are agreements between parents and children that describe goals and set realistic expectations on how to meet those goals. If the goals are attained, the child gets a reward. In most cases, there is one contract that serves both the parents and the child, but it may be useful for parents to sign a separate agreement, in the presence of the child, to show their commitment to this undertaking. A parent contract can include the amount of time the parent agrees to spend with the child during each homework session and the number of times per week the parent commits to working with the child. There may also be a list of goals for the child and a signed agreement that the parent will grant rewards (daily, weekly, or long-term) if the child attains the stated goals. Following are examples of a parent-and-child homework contract and a child homework contract. Your child's homework contract should include what goals you want him to attain and what specific behaviors or habits must be followed. Goals may consist of bringing home assignments and books needed, achieving a certain grade on homework, writing down all homework assignments, completing homework within a specified time frame, and so on. The contract should also spell out rewards that will be earned with appropriate behaviors.

Sample Parent-and-Child Homework Contract

This homework contract will help you define your role as a "coach" in the homework process. Sit down with your child and talk about what a contract is. Explain that it is a promise in writing. Talk about the daily and weekly rewards that your child can earn. These rewards should be reasonable and not too time-consuming. Some choices are rewards that do not cost money and are easy to carry out. Keep a weekly contract stating what you as the parent promise to do and what your child promises to do.

Week of: _____

Parent or guardian's section:

_____ I checked my child's homework.

_____ I provided assistance and did not give out answers.

_____ I gave a daily reward for homework achievement (circle the days):   Mon   Tue   Wed   Thu   Fri

Child's section:

Write the goals for the week that you need to work on:

    1.   Writing down correct homework assignment daily: _____

    2.   Finishing homework by my bedtime: _____

    3.   Not forgetting homework at home: _____

Possible daily rewards:

    1.   Extra 15 minutes of TV or computer: _____

    2.   Bedtime extended by 15 minutes: _____

    3.   Extra outside play: _____

Possible weekly rewards:

    1.   See a movie: _____

    2.   Get to stay up late on Saturday night: _____

    3.   Have a friend over for a play date: _____

Parent's signature: _____ Child's signature: _____

Sample Student Homework Contract

Sit down with your child and talk about what your child needs to target with homework. Write these down as goals. Work on achieving 90 percent of the goals weekly.

Goal:

I will:

Bring homework assignments home.

Complete homework in each subject.

Finish homework before 8:00 P.M.

Have teacher sign weekly sheet indicating all homework was completed.

Receive a grade of 80 or better on all assignments.

Signature: _____ Date: _____

Percent goal achieved: _____

Monday: _____

Tuesday: _____

Wednesday: _____

Thursday: _____

Friday: _____

Average weekly percent goal achieved: _____

Possible daily rewards:

Ice cream or treat; extra television, telephone, or computer time.

Possible weekly rewards:

Video or movie rental; having a friend spend the night; going out to eat.

Possible monthly rewards:

New video game; piece of clothing or accessory; CD; DVD

Possible long-term rewards:

Party with friends; new outfit; new toy

Snapshot #43:

How Important Is Extra Credit?

My child is constantly faced with extra-credit questions or assignments. Her teacher believes that the extra credit is a good thing; I think it just adds more stress and keeps my child from extracurricular activities. My child hates doing them and I don't see it as necessary. I am just glad when my child has completed her projects and homework on time. What should I do?

Tip : Arrange for a conference and find out the teacher's view on extra credit. Obviously she views it as a good activity since she always includes it with the course work. The teacher probably assigns the extra credit as a time for your child to utilize higher-level skills and develop advanced thinking. If your child has difficulty and is getting frustrated, let her stop. I would definitely encourage your daughter to try. It can only increase her learning potential. You may want to include it as part of a homework contract: "I tried the extra-credit question."

www.School-talk.com

Snapshot #44:
I Need a Homework Success Plan

s a parent, I believe that when my child does homework it increases her knowledge. Lately I have been getting frustrated as my daughter keeps putting off her assignments. Her bedtime is 9:00 P.M., and many times she still has not started her homework. I am tired of nagging. What should I do?

> *Successful homework plans are often joint efforts, with both parents and children striving for academic achievement.*

Tip : You and your daughter can join forces to conquer the homework issues that are so often part of the struggles in today's families. Both of you need to have open communication about why education is important, how homework is valuable, and the difficulties and frustrations in doing the assignments. After there is some open talk, then you both can devise plans to alleviate difficulties.

A successful homework plan involves strategies for doing homework effectively and efficiently. You both need to agree on how much time each night is devoted to schoolwork. It is often helpful for parents and children—depending on the age of the child—to agree on time parameters. For instance, most parents don't feel comfortable allowing their child to stay up until midnight to finish homework, but many children have activities that prevent them from doing homework early in the evening. A compromise might be reached where a child has until 9:00 P.M. to finish homework. Other strategies may include specifying that the most difficult subject be done first, or that every subject have some time devoted to it. Homework contracts may be valuable in offering rewards for successful completion of goals, and parents should review their child's completed assignments.

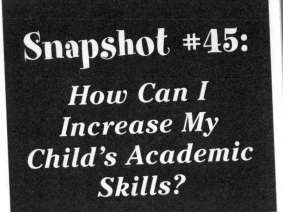

Snapshot #45:

How Can I Increase My Child's Academic Skills?

Homework contracts are beneficial to keep a child on track. They allow all parties—teacher, parent, and child—to know exactly what is expected and what needs to be done. Following are two examples of contracts for success.

I know I play a large part in helping my child achieve academic success. I do whatever I can to support the teacher and the work she assigns, but I'd like to do more. What should I do?

Tip : A parent can be helpful in many, many ways. Always know what your child is studying at school. Whenever possible, talk about it. Explain to your child what you do at your job and all the various kinds of skills you employ in doing it. Talk to your child about history, politics, music, art, and society in general. Show your child how big the world is and how much there is to know. Read! Read! Read!—anything and everything, from newspapers, to magazines, to novels. If your child sees you reading, she will be much more likely to view it as a desirable activity. If you read to your child, you will be teaching her vocabulary and different writing techniques as well as spending valuable time together. There is a definite correlation between the amount of time a child spends reading and academic success. (Think about it: If you've read a lot, somehow the conventions of grammar and spelling come naturally to you. If you haven't been exposed to good writing, how will you ever know how to do it? Plus, think of all you learn from reading!) Don't forget the old standby instructional methods: flash cards, videos, and books. Go to the library. A positive, upbeat, supportive attitude about schools, the teachers, the programs, and education in general is a priceless commodity in promoting a child's academic success.

Sample Parent Contract for Academic Success

Sit with your child and discuss what a contract is. A contract is a written promise.

    I, _____, the [mother/father] of _____, promise that I will promote the success of my child by providing the following help:

_____ I will provide a quiet, clean, study area for my child.

_____ I will provide materials needed for homework assignments:

    _____ Pencils/pens

    _____ Lined paper/construction paper

    _____ Scissors

    _____ Glue/paste

    _____ Dictionary/thesaurus

    _____ Maps/atlas

    _____ Ruler

    _____ Markers/crayons/colored pencils/watercolors

_____ I will set up an appropriate daily homework routine.

_____ I will monitor study time and assist my child with homework questions.

_____ I will keep track of my child's progress through any or all of the following methods:

    _____ Keeping in contact with the teacher

    _____ Using a progress tracker

    _____ Reviewing the homework assignment book

    _____ Checking the backpack nightly

_____ I will remind my child to prepare the backpack for the next day.

Signed: _____   Date: _____

Sample Child Contract for Academic Success

I, _____, the _____ of _____, promise that I will work to succeed in school by doing the following activities:

_____ Each day, I will write down all the assignments given by the teacher.

_____ I will ask questions about any homework assignments I don't understand.

_____ I will bring home the books I need each night.

_____ I will do my homework in the special homework area provided for me.

_____ I will follow a daily homework routine established by my parents.

_____ I will do the work on time, not playing around when I'm supposed to be studying.

_____ I will tell the truth about assignments and grades.

_____ I will put all the finished assignments in my backpack for the next day when I finish.

Signed: _____

Date: _____

Your Homework Assignment: The Homework Contract

Directions: Now that you have completed this chapter, take some time to answer the following questions. This is a short assignment that will act as review and, we hope, increase your understating of key points.

1. Write a homework contract for your child.

2. List three ways you can help your child at home during homework time.

    a.

    b.

    c.

3. What is your role in the homework process?

CHAPTER FIVE
It's All About Homework

"This one step, choosing a goal and sticking to it, changes everything."
Scott Reed

By now you can see how important homework is to your child's academic success. The following scenarios will summarize the valuable points that have been spotlighted throughout this book. Help your child become self-motivated, responsible, self-directed, and organized by using the important tools outlined in this chapter, including these:

- Implementing a reward system
- Relating homework to the real world
- Planning a homework schedule together
- Keeping a calendar of projects and assignments
- Setting realistic goals

Snapshot #46:

How Can I Help My Child Become More Self-Motivated About Homework?

Do all children fight the idea of homework as much as my daughter does? She finds every excuse in the book to avoid sitting down and doing her assignments. I want to help her become self-motivated. I have to either threaten or bribe her to get her to do her homework. What should I do?

Organized people are often the most self-motivated!

Tip: Rest assured, your daughter is like most other children—not to mention most adults! It's difficult to sit down and work when you have options that are much more pleasurable and much less demanding. However, it's important that your child learn self-motivation, a quality attained through coaching, example, and practice.

You'll need to encourage your daughter by showing her how to sit down and work on a task. You might consider sitting with her and doing some work of your own while she does her homework. Whether it's balancing a checkbook, writing a letter, paying bills, or writing out a grocery list, you'll be showing her that you can get work accomplished fairly quickly when you just "do it." Talk to her about how good you feel when you have completed a small job. Help her recognize the pride she feels when she has accomplished what she set out to do. In teaching motivation, it's helpful to set a daily schedule with designated times for homework or chores. Another often-used strategy to help children become self-motivated is to offer a reward of some sort. For example, if she completes her homework within a certain time frame, then she gets a prize. This tangible acknowledgment of her hard work will foster repeat behavior in the future.

Snapshot #47:

How Can I Help My Child Become More Responsible About Homework?

I get frustrated by my son's irresponsibility. He is a sixth-grader, yet he doesn't remember assignments, never puts things away, and rarely does what I ask him to do without several reminders. Homework is certainly not a priority. I want to teach him to act more responsibly. What should I do?

Tip : As we know, children aren't born being responsible, so like anything else, parents and teachers have to model that trait for it to be learned. If your child really is oblivious to the necessities of homework, explain to him why homework is assigned: He might need more time to practice an idea, he might need to make sure he can do it without help, he might need time to think about it and apply it to other situations. Give him real examples of how this homework topic is used in the outside world on a daily basis.

My mother's words have stayed with me for a lifetime: "With privilege goes responsibility." It may be time to teach your son the very real-world concept of cause and effect. Be specific in identifying the good behaviors: "Because you remembered to bring home assignments and then completed the work on time, you get the privilege of staying up a half hour later than usual." "Because you acted responsibly, studied for the math test, and earned a B (choose whatever grade you deem necessary for your situation), you've earned the privilege of going out to eat at the restaurant of your choice." The idea is that the more your son sees the benefits of responsible behavior, the more likely he is to act in that manner.

www.school-talk.com

Snapshot #48:

How Can I Help My Child Become More Independent About Homework?

My wife and I work different shifts. I'm the one at home at night with our three children, ages six, ten, and fourteen, so homework duty falls on my shoulders. They all seem to need help each night with their homework, but I can't possibly be with each one of them every minute of the evening helping them on every assignment. I want to make them more independent and self-directed with their homework. What should I do?

Tip: You may have to spend a few minutes with each child at the beginning of the homework time. Make sure you have an open work space with all the necessary pens, pencils, papers, staplers, markers, and whatever else they need, so there are no interruptions once they sit down to work. Give each child five minutes of undivided attention, asking each one what kind of assignments are required, which subject is the hardest, what work will take the longest to complete. From there, help your children develop a plan for the evening. Together, plot out how much time they'll spend on each topic and aim for a time to have the work completed. Many experts suggest starting with the most difficult topic or the one that will take the longest, so that the student has the necessary energy and concentration to tackle the work. Check back with each child every half hour and review their work when completed.

Although you don't have to hover over your children, you can still make sure they know that if absolutely stumped, they can come to you for help. The trick here is to find the balance between doing too much to help them and making sure they direct their own activity.

And again, a proven technique for increasing motivation and self-reliance is the reward system. Tell them when everyone finishes their homework, you'll all play a board game or have pizza.

Snapshot #49:

How Can Homework Make My Child Become Better Organized?

I struggle daily with my daughter who says things like "I didn't know I needed it today" or "I thought I would finish it tomorrow." I want to help her focus on her homework and her organizational skills. What should I do?

www.school-talk.com

Tip: No matter the age of the child, it's never too early to teach organizational skills. You can teach your child to plan homework activities and pay attention to deadlines through several methods. First, every day, remind her to look at her journal/planner and her calendar to see what is due the next day. You might have a section on the monthly calendar that reminds her of major events or projects coming up.

It's easy to find blank monthly calendars that you can print out. At the beginning of the month give her a blank calendar. Have her write in the dates of projects, field trips, tests, and so on. Post this on the refrigerator where everyone can view it and where she can easily add to it as a new assignment is given. It's a documented fact that the act of writing promotes memory and learning, so she will be more likely to remember the dates on her calendar. And by making her own individual calendar, she will take ownership.

Always provide time at the end of each day to review homework assignments together. Make this part of your family routine. Second, teach your child the skill of making lists. Every night, ask your daughter to make a list of all the items she will need the next day and to spend just a few moments making sure all the necessary supplies are in her backpack. You may want to photocopy lists with boxes she can check for those items needed (pencils, lunch money, books, scissors, notes).

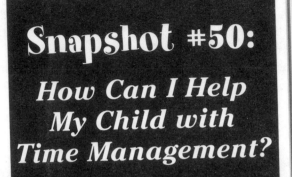

Snapshot #50:

How Can I Help My Child with Time Management?

My daughter is always rushing around at the last minute to finish assignments. I don't know whether she just procrastinates or whether it takes her too long to complete the work. I want to help her manage her time better. What should I do?

Time management can be learned!

Tip : There's no doubt that doing homework can be a valuable lesson in time management. If your daughter is a true procrastinator—meaning she would just prefer to do her work later rather than sooner—you can fix that by enforcing a scheduled homework time. If she completes her work during the requisite time period, she can earn a reward. However, sometimes there are specific problems that cause someone to procrastinate. If she puts off doing her work because she has a hard time focusing, have her work on one or two questions at a time and then take a short break. If she has a short attention span, it might help to let her switch from subject to subject. Perhaps she procrastinates because she really hates a certain subject. If so, work with her on an effective strategy, whether it's doing just a few problems at a time, doing all the work and then earning a big segment of free time, or doing one problem and then moving to a topic she likes. Make sure that you work with her on a plan to get her homework done. Try breaking down the assignments into smaller tasks to be accomplished during assigned segments of time, with a guaranteed reward. For instance, if she finishes her math within a half hour, then she will earn extra computer time.

Snapshot #51:

How Can I Help My Child Avoid Frustration?

www.School-talk.com

My son doesn't do well with any homework assignment that involves reading and writing. Every night when we make him sit down and work, he becomes short-tempered and irritable and often acts out angrily. He quickly gets frustrated with the work and it's difficult to get him to finish anything. What should I do?

Tip : As parents, we hurt when our child hurts, but don't despair. There are several things that you can do to help ease your son's frustration. First, speak to the teacher about your concerns. Ask whether he also acts like this at school and if the teacher is aware of any underlying problems that would contribute to this behavior.

Second, consider the possibility that physiological problems might be the cause of his frustration. You may want to have his eyesight and hearing checked or have him tested for a learning disorder.

Third, and most important, encourage him. Let him know you think he is a wonderful person and a good student. Tell him no one knows everything and all learning is a process. Reassure him that you are there to help him, then follow through by working with him each evening and coaching him through his homework. While you don't want to do his work for him, you can help by answering questions or giving him examples. And again, implement a reward system—one that offers daily rewards as well as bigger, long-term rewards when he completes homework efficiently and without protest.

Snapshot #52:

How Does Homework Boost Academic Performance?

The most beneficial homework is focused on real-life learning.

M y husband and I have disagreements over the amount of time our children should spend on homework versus the amount of time to spend on sports activities and musical lessons. He says that the real-world skills and abilities derived from sports and music are more important than the often "frivolous" homework assigned by teachers. I say that homework is essential to our children doing well in school. What should I do?

Tip : Balance is the key to everything in life. Your husband is right in that athletic strength and physical fitness are extraordinarily important assets. Kids benefit from the concepts of practice and teamwork, and in this day when the media openly discusses the crisis of obesity, no one doubts the need for physical activity. Musical training, too, is a skill that will benefit a person for a lifetime, an ability well worth the investment of time and energy. But you are right in that homework DOES improve a child's comprehension, particularly when children are at the junior high age or older. While homework assignments may seem "frivolous" or "trivial" at times, research shows that students who do homework significantly raise their test scores and their class rankings. Doing homework promotes mastery of necessary skills, making each progressive lesson easier to understand. Time management, organizational skills, self-discipline, and self-reliance are also promoted by frequent homework completion. The best homework is more than just fill-in-the-blank worksheets. Your husband and you should come to an agreement about how many nights per week are spent in activities outside of academics, and how much time per night is spent doing homework and school projects.

Your Homework Assignment: It's All About Homework

Directions: Now that you have completed Chapter Five, take some time to answer the following questions. This is a short assignment that will act as a review and, we hope, increase your understanding of the key points.

1. What techniques do you use to make your child more responsible?

2. How do you use rewards and consequences to increase your child's homework success?

3. How do you help your child become better organized?

4. List two ways you can help your child to become self-motivated.

   a.

   b.

APPENDIX A

Secrets for a Smarter Child Revealed: Learning Styles

"Yesterday I dared to struggle. Today I dared to win."
Bernadette Devlin

What Is YOUR Child's Learning Style?

To better understand your children and how they think, it is important to know their learning style. Every child is unique and has at least one strong learning style; many tend to have more than one. Children learn at different rates and in different ways. Do you want to help your child become smarter, reduce stress in school, and have a happy life? Are you ready to determine your child's learning style? Ready, set, go!

The Seven Learning Styles

First, let's go over the seven learning styles. Child psychologists will tell you that there are a variety of learning styles, categorized in a multitude of ways. To simplify this concept, educators and psychologists have drawn out seven different types of learning styles. Your child may have one or two or even more of these styles. Realizing your child's strengths and weaknesses is an important step all parents should take to maximize their child's potential. If your child has a weakness in a certain subject area because of a particular learning style, you can assist your child and work with the teacher and the school to overcome this weakness. Taking this step can make a world of difference in a child's success.

Linguistic

Linguistic learners love language in written or verbal format. They learn more quickly through storytelling, poetry, and abstract examples. They are easily captivated by stories that have rhythmic words or tones in them. They are attentive during storytelling times.

Mathematical

Mathematical learners love to observe, analyze, and create patterns. They like to sort things out and organize their resources, and they reason with numbers and sequences. They enjoy step-by-step processes.

www.School-talk.com

Physical or Kinesthetic

Physical or kinesthetic learners are children who can never sit still. These children learn by movements or physical activities. One of the best ways for a physical learner to learn is to literally get his hands on the activity, better known as "hands-on learning."

Intrapersonal

Intrapersonal learners are usually mistaken as loners or antisocial. What makes them unique is their ability to absorb information by themselves, through independent reading, research, and exploring the Internet. They enjoy journal writing and goal setting.

Interpersonal

Interpersonal learners love to talk to people. They love to be helpers, are quite social, and prove to be great team players. They enjoy "speaking out" on their ideas and opinions. They absorb information and learn best when they are in groups or work with a buddy, as they are proven to be good talkers and good listeners.

Musical

Musical learners are vibrant, rhythmic, and melodic. They respond well to tunes and can easily remember or memorize songs and jingles. They absorb information through sounds and music. They can work on their studies with soft background music (not pop music); in fact, the soft music helps them stay focused.

Visual

Visual learners are artistic. They absorb information through pictures, diagrams, maps, and charts. Visual children enjoy drawing and coloring, and they pay great attention to detail. Visual learners are imaginative and creative, and they work well with their hands.

The following activities may help you discover your child's learning style.

Your Child's Learning Style

Find your child's learning style by reviewing the following statements. Check the boxes with those items that describe your child's preferences.

Linguistic Child:

My child loves to read stories of all kinds. ☐

My child loves to listen to stories and rhymes. ☐

My child loves to read and listen to poems and riddles. ☐

My child is attentive during reading and language arts sessions. ☐

My child is inattentive during math and science classes. ☐

My child loves to read street signs, billboards, cereal boxes, and so on. ☐

Linguistic score: ___ out of 6

Mathematical Child:

My child loves to arrange patterns in sequences. ☐

My child loves to count different objects in different ways. ☐

My child can easily remember numbers, such as phone numbers. ☐

My child likes to sort out objects by color, style, or size. ☐

My child is attentive during math sessions. ☐

My child is inattentive during language arts or reading sessions. ☐

Mathematical score: ___ out of 6

Physical Child:

My child loves to move around rather than to stay still. ☐

My child fidgets when he reads or writes in class. ☐

My child loves to touch objects and animals. ☐

My child loves to play physical games and prefers the outdoors. ☐

My child loves to dance and move around at any sound of music. ☐

My child has a hard time sitting or standing still. ☐

Physical score: ___out of 6

Intrapersonal Child:

My child works well alone. ☐

My child reads independently. ☐

My child works on his assignments independently. ☐

My child is quiet and shy. ☐

My child doesn't like to socialize much. ☐

My child enjoys playing alone. ☐

Intrapersonal score: ___ out of 6

Interpersonal Child:

My child dislikes to work or study alone. ☐

My child likes to be in a group of children. ☐

My child is known to be friendly in school. ☐

My child likes to help other people and gets very concerned about others. ☐

My child is a good talker. ☐

My child can strike up a conversation with just about anyone. ☐

Interpersonal score: ___ out of 6

Musical Child:

My child knows most lyrics of popular songs and jingles. ☐

My child loves music. ☐

My child loves to sing. ☐

My child can read a book with different intonations. ☐

My child likes to create music with everyday objects, such as pots and pans. ☐

My child hums most of the time. ☐

Musical score: ___ out of 6

Visual Child:

My child looks out for the tiniest details in a picture. ☐

My child loves to play with blocks and other building toys. ☐

My child loves to work on puzzles or mazes. ☐

My child loves to color, draw, and doodle. ☐

My child enjoys looking at diagrams, maps, and charts. ☐

My child loves to watch slide shows and videos. ☐

Visual score: ___ out of 6

Place the number for each of the following categories:

_____ LINGUISTIC

_____ MATHEMATICAL

_____ PHYSICAL

_____ INTRAPERSONAL

_____ INTERPERSONAL

_____ MUSICAL

_____ VISUAL

Into which category did most of your checkmarks fall? Your child's primary learning style will be the category that has the highest score. Your child can have more than one primary learning style. Your child's secondary learning style is the category that has the second highest score.

Remember, every individual has at least one primary learning style. As a parent, familiarizing yourself with your child's learning style can allow you to bring out your child's personal best.

Source: www.Eduville.com

Learning Style Worksheet

From information learned when completing the preceding worksheet, fill in the blanks to customize your child's own personalized learning style. If your child has more than one learning style, you may want to list the most frequently used one first.

My child's main learning style is:

_____

My child's other learning style (if applicable) is:

_____

My child needs to strengthen the following:

1. _____

2. _____

Source: www.Eduville.com

APPENDIX B
Resources and References

Web Sites

The following Web sites offer help with homework.

About.com

Provides links to articles and resources on a variety of learning tools, including those for helping with homework.

Ed.gov

The Department of Education offers publications and information for parents on help with homework and other educational issues.

Discoveryschool.com

Reviews products, gives advice, offers study tools, and lists resources.

Eduville.com

An educational learning village to assist parents with school success.

Executiveparent.com

Focuses on information and advice that supports parent involvement in their children's success.

Familyeducation.com

Provides school solutions, homework help, parenting tips, and expert advice.

IdealLives.com

The Ideal Lives Inclusion & Advocacy Center is an online community that supports parents raising children with special needs. It offers a weekly newsletter, an easy-to-use research center of practical resources, an article library filled with expert advice on every category of special education, news updates on special education and disability topics and learning opportunities, and the opportunity to connect with other parents facing similar challenges.

KidsHealth.com

Gives information, guidance, and resources written specifically for three target groups: younger kids, teens, and parents.

PTA.org

Supports parents and teachers through a national network of programs.

School-Talk.com

A site for communication and school success.

Link

For more information on the correlation between homework and academic success, check out the following:

http://www.ferndale.wednet.edu/custer/FAQs/homework.html

You'll find the homework policies, calendar, and guidelines of an actual elementary school, which parents and teachers can use to create their own homework contracts, and so on.

Books

You may also find the following books to be helpful.

Ending the Homework Hassle, by John Rosemond (Kansas City, Mo.: Andrews and McMeel Publishing, 1990)

Homework Wars, by Marguerite C. Radencich and Jeanne Shay Schumm (Minneapolis: Free Spirit Publishing, rev. ed., 1996)

Homework Without Tears, by Lee Canter (New York: HarperCollins, 2005)

How to Do Homework Without Throwing Up, by Trevor Romain (Minneapolis: Free Spirit Publishing, 1997)

How to Help Your Child with Homework: The Complete Guide to Encouraging Good Study Habits and Ending the Homework Wars, Rev. ed., by Jeanne Shay Schumm (Minneapolis: Free Spirit Publishing, 2005)

Overcoming Underachieving: A Simple Plan to Boost Your Kids' Grades and Their Homework Hassles, by Ruth Allen Peters (New York: Broadway Books, 2000)

Seven Steps to Homework Success: A Family Guide to Solving Common Homework Problems, by Sydney Zentall and Sam Goldstein (Plantation, Fla.: Specialty Press, 1998)

Homework Clubs

Many schools across the country have established homework clubs, providing a space for students to work, offering access to resources and materials, and bringing in volunteers as advisers and mentors. Check with the school principal and counselor about how to develop your own homework club.

APPENDIX C

Parent Involvement: Learning Fun Collection

It's easy to find many opportunities during the day, evening, or weekend to do fun activities that can increase learning and studying skills, as well as enhance family togetherness. On the following pages you will find some learning games that can be played at home, while taking a walk, or during car pool. They are fun experiences for you and your child and at the same time provide opportunities for learning.

Summer Vacation Family Activities

Everyone's a Star! (Elementary Age)

Each night take turns reading aloud from a book; it can be several pages or just a page or two. Make reading fun by inviting siblings to participate or rotating the activity, such as you and your child (and others) reading alternating pages, paragraphs, or sentences. When you've finished the story, decide if your children want to put on a performance. Every member who reads part of the story takes on a role, and the readers put on a show for friends or other members of the family. Make a list of who will take which part, what each

performer will wear, and then write the script. Plan this out—start to finish—as a family. You might even want to turn this into a math project by planning a budget for the cost of props, costumes, and refreshments.

Plan Your Summer Television Schedule (Elementary Age)

Tell your child that you intend to limit television viewing each day. Discuss viewing times and options together. Once you decide the amount of viewing time allowed per day, have your child search the television guide or TV section of the newspaper. Let him fill out the following weekly chart, then you enforce the schedule. Restrict choices to those programs you consider appropriate; encourage viewing programs on an educational channel.

www.school-talk.com

Sample: Summer Television Schedule

Channel	Sunday	Monday	Tuesday	Wednesday	Thursday	Friday	Saturday
2	Arthur 30 minutes						
TVL	Mr. Ed 30 minutes						
Disney	Movie 2 hours						
Total time each day	3 hours						

Weekend Family Fun Time (Any Age)

Plan ahead. Look in the newspapers to find fun events and write down the things you and the family will do together over the summer.

Keeping a Daily Log: What I Did This Summer (Any Age)

Print up a monthly blank calendar. Depending on your child's age, have him write a few words or sentences on how HE spent each day, including weekends.

Step Up Your Vocabulary (Any Age)

Get a new index card box in which 5- by 7-inch index cards will fit. Buy at least two packages of cards—any color you wish. While you are at the store, buy new markers and/or pens. Then get ready! Every day, while reading a newspaper article or book, have your child pick out a word he has never read before. Then have him take out an index card and write the word on one side of it. On the other side write the definition, then create a sentence that uses the new word. He may want to draw a small picture to illustrate the word. This will help him remember it. When he is finished, have him put the card into the word index box and practice reading it every night before going to bed. Imagine how many new words he will have by the time school starts again.

www.school-talk.com

Sample: Weekend Family Fun Time

Dates	Saturday	Sunday
July 3-4	See new Disney movie.	See fireworks at the local city park.

Sample: What I Did This Summer

Week of (Date)	Sunday	Monday	Tuesday	Wednesday	Thursday	Friday	Saturday
July 1	I went to friend's house to swim.	Camp: Went on a trip to the zoo.	Camp: Went for a boat ride.	No Camp: Family went to the beach and had a picnic for July 4.	Camp: Had a parade and picnic.	Camp: Did a great arts and crafts project—made a jewelry box out of popsicle sticks.	Family went to the movies and out to eat at my favorite restaurant.
July 8	Went to Grandma's house and she had homemade ice cream.						

School Year Family Activities

The Night Before School Starts (Kindergarten through Second Grade)

The child fills out the right-hand column of the following chart with how she feels the night before school starts. A parent fills out the left-hand column. Look it over and compare. You might be surprised at each other's feelings. Some will be similar and others might be very different. Talk about them. It helps to understand how every member in the family feels about things that are happening to one another. Writing them down helps begin a conversation.

Feelings (Any Age)

Everyone has great days and not such super-duper days. With a family member's help, have your child try this activity. Have her write down what happened during the day that made her unhappy or angry. Sometimes writing it down helps organize your thoughts and brings understanding. Now ask your child to think about what she could do the next time this happens so her day will go better.

Safety First (Pre-Kindergarten Through Second Grade)

Take a walk with your child and give him safety tips, such as:

- "Look both ways before crossing the street."
- "See that bike rider? He's wearing a helmet. It's important to wear a helmet when riding a bike."
- "We have to wait for the hand on the sign to turn green before we can cross the street."
- "Hear the siren? Notice how the cars are slowing down and stopping. It's not a good idea to go into the road until the emergency vehicle passes."
- "Hold my hand. That man over there is a stranger."

When you get back home, ask your child to try to remember five rules he learned on the walk. Have him write one on a piece of paper and then draw a picture for each safety rule. Then staple all the pages together to make a book.

The Night Before School Starts

Parent's Side	Child's Side
1.	1.
2.	2.
3.	3.
Extra thoughts:	Extra thoughts:

Sample: My Feelings

Not-So-Great Day	How to Have a Great Day
1. Forgot my homework and the teacher wrote my name on the board.	1. Stick to my routine and put my homework in the homework folder and then in my backpack the night before.
2. Got five problems wrong on a math practice sheet.	2. Review my work a little each night and do my homework carefully because it has practice examples that are always on my teacher's tests.
3. My best friend didn't sit next to me at lunch.	3. Ask before lunch if my friend would sit next to me.

Sharpen Your Visual Skills and Become a Good Investigator (Elementary Age)

Go outside, somewhere around your neighborhood. Go to the mall, the library, or a fast-food restaurant with your child. Find a spot to sit down, maybe on a park bench or in the outside dining patio of a restaurant. Look around you, then decide on an area that both of you will watch for five minutes. Each of you needs a piece of paper, a pen or pencil, and something flat to write on. Pick three or four things you will be looking for while you're sitting there, such as animals, dogs on a leash, babies in strollers, people wearing hats, joggers, yellow cars, and so on. Jot down a description of each pertinent sighting. Compare your lists after the time is up.

Family Scrapbook (Any Age, Including Adults)

Fill in pages with photos starting with your ancestors to the present. Along with pictures, include some of the activities that follow, plus report cards, poetry, drawings, awards—anything family members would like to contribute. You and your family will learn much about your ancestors, their background, world history, your own culture, and the culture of other countries. Your family will spend many enjoyable hours together on this project, and the result will be a wonderful family keepsake.

Family Tree (Entire Family)

Have your family create a family tree tracing your ancestors. Include the names of parents, grandparents, aunts, uncles, and so on. Include the place and date of birth for everyone and date of death for those who have died. Draw a tree or cut out a picture of a tree from a magazine. If you don't want to draw, you may wish to trace one from a book or download one from the Internet. On each branch, put a family member's last name and on the leaves of that branch place their children's names and all the information mentioned here.

Where Is My Family From? (Entire Family)

Now that you've asked where everyone came from, look up those countries. Draw their flags and place them on a map. Find two interesting facts about each country, such as kinds of food, what crops they grow, what holidays they celebrate, the climate, and so on.

Time Line (Entire Family)

Once you have all the birth dates, start a time line on which your child places the name of each family member and the year everyone was born. Watch the line get longer and longer with each new birth.

Sharpen Your Visual Skills and Become a Good Investigator

How Many the Child Spotted	Child's Description	How Many the Parent Spotted	Parent's Description

Family Ancestry Treasure Hunt (All Ages)

Have your child go around your house and find items that represent your culture. He should ask you about them and take down the information. He may even want to take a picture of these items for another page in the family scrapbook.

Family Interviews (All Ages)

Have your child write questions that he would like to ask your relatives about their lives and what they remember about their parents. Then have him gather the information and write a short story about each relative. Get a photograph and place it with the interview. Put it all into the family scrapbook.

All-About-Me Interview (All Ages)

Have your child think of questions she would like to answer, providing information to share with the other members of the family that tells them all about her (see the examples that follow). She might like to include both a baby picture and a current picture of herself. This too can go into the family scrapbook, along with the family interviews.

www.school-talk.com

Family Ancestry Treasure Hunt

1. Item found: _____
   Describe the item.

   Describe how it is used in your culture.

   Explain why it's important.

2. Item found: _____
   Describe the item.

   Describe how it is used in your culture.

   Explain why it's important.

Family Interview Sheet

Name of person interviewed: _____

Date: _____

1. What country were you born in?

2. What country did your parents come from?

3. What language did your parents speak?

4. What languages do you speak?

5. What are some of your favorite foods that come from the country you or your ancestors come from? Please share the recipe(s) with us.

6. What holidays did your parents teach you about?

7. Which holiday is your favorite and how do you celebrate it?

8. Tell me about something you want to share with the rest of the family that is important to our family history.

All-About-Me Interview

Name: _____

Date: _____

1. Name the people in your family and their ages.

2. List your pets if you have any.

3. What are your favorite foods?

4. What is your favorite thing to do with your family?

5. What is your best family event memory?

6. What is your favorite holiday and how do you celebrate it?

7. Write a story all about "You."

Members of a Family Are Alike and Different (All Ages)

Ask your child to observe you and your spouse over several days. He should study how you look, speak, stand, what you like and dislike, and so on, and then fill out the following chart. Younger children may need your help.

Everyone Keeps to a Schedule (Entire Family)

Have everyone in the family sit down and fill out their daily schedule. This will help everyone keep track of the things they need to do, as well as the time the family can spend together. It will also help your child understand that everyone has jobs to

do. Right now, the child's job is to attend school and do the best work he can.

Rules to Live By (All Ages)

Fill in the following chart with the rules you have as a family and then review them together. Each member might have additions and corrections. The goal is to come up with one chart that everyone can agree on.

Members of a Family Are Alike and Different

I am the same as my mom because:

1. _____

2. _____

3. _____

I am different from my mom because:

1. _____

2. _____

3. _____

I am the same as my dad because:

1. _____

2. _____

3. _____

I am different from my dad because:

1. _____

2. _____

3. _____

Sample: Everyone Keeps to a Schedule

Time	Child's Activities	Time	One Parent's Activities
6:00 A.M.	Eat breakfast.	6:00 A.M.	Eat breakfast.
7:15 A.M.	Leave for school.	7:15 A.M.	Drive to school.
8:00 A.M.–5:30 P.M.	In school.	8:00 A.M.–5:00 P.M.	At work.
		5:30 P.M.	Pick up at school.
5:30–6:30 P.M.	Watch television.	5:30–6:30 P.M.	Prepare dinner.
6:30–7:00 P.M.	Eat dinner.	6:30–7:00 P.M.	Eat dinner.
7:00–8:00 P.M.	Do homework.	7:00–7:30 P.M.	Clean up.
8:00–8:30 P.M.	Get ready for bed.	7:30–8:30 P.M.	Read and relax.
8:30–9:00 P.M.	Read.	8:30–9:00 P.M.	Read with my child.
9:00 P.M.	Bedtime.	11:00 P.M.	Bedtime.

Rules to Live By

School Rules	House Rules	Rules for Friends When They Visit
1.	1.	1.
2.	2.	2.
3.	3.	3.
4.	4.	4.
5.	5.	5.

Learning Games for Car Travel (Elementary Age)

1. *I Spy:* Say "I spy" followed by something your child should look for out the window. Once he "spies" it, he takes a turn finding something. He must answer in a complete sentence.

   Example: "I spy something yellow." "Is it the yellow school bus?"

2. *Alphabet Animal* (or use types of cars, people's names, countries, cities, and so on): If you pick animals, you start by saying "A is for Ant." Your child then says "B is for Bat (or Buffalo)." It then becomes your turn again until you reach the end of the alphabet.

3. *Places:* One person names a country or famous place—for example, America. The next person has to name a country, city, or famous place that begins with the last letter of the previous place named. In this case America ends in A, so the next person can say "Antarctica," "Albany," or "Atlantis." If it's "Atlantis," then the next place would start with the letter S, which could be Switzerland or Seattle, and so on, until someone gets stuck.

www.school-talk.com

About
the Authors

About Cheli Cerra

For more than 18 years, she has helped thousands of children achieve school and life success. As a school principal and a mother of two, Cheli knows firsthand the issues that teachers, parents, and children face. She was the founding principal of one of the first K–8 schools in Miami-Dade County, Florida, Everglades Elementary. The school of 1,500 students received an A+ rating from the Florida Department of Education for two consecutive years under Cheli's leadership.

Cheli is the founder of Eduville, Inc., a company that provides resources and strategies for parents and teachers to help their children achieve school and life success. Among her resources are Smarter Kid Secrets, a free monthly e-zine, and her website http://www.eduville.com, full of tips, techniques, and strategies useful for anyone interested in helping a child succeed. Cheli serves on the Florida Advisory Board for GreatSchools.net, a nonprofit, online guide to K-12 education.

Recognized as "The Right Choice" by *Woman's Day* magazine, and featured on over 30 radio shows throughout the country, Cheli is committed to helping teachers and parents come together for the success of children. Her seminars, coaching programs, and presentations have provided strategies that empower her audiences to action. She will captivate you by teaching the lessons learned from her in-the-trenches experience in public education. As a wife and a working mother of two, she understands the reality of everyday life and creates strategies to meet these challenges quickly and easily. Her powerful message of immigrating to this country, learning the language, and adapting to a new culture also give Cheli a unique insight to the real-world challenges children face today.

Co-creator of the School-Talk Success Series: *Teacher Talk!*, *Parent Talk!*, *School Board Talk!*, and *Principal Talk!* For more information, go to http://www.school-talk.com.

About Dr. Ruth Jacoby

Dr. Ruth is the founding principal of the Somerset Academy charter schools, which include five charter schools with 1,250 students in prekindergarten through tenth grade. She has more than 30 years of experience as an administrator and educator, in traditional public, private, and charter schools. Under her leadership, Somerset Charter School became one of the first charter schools to receive SACS (Southern Association of Colleges and Schools) accreditation. Her middle school received an A+ rating from the Florida Department of Education in its first year of operation.

Dr. Ruth received her Ed.D. degree in Child and Youth Studies for Children from Birth through 18 Years from Nova Southeastern University, and her Master of Science in Special Needs and Bachelor of Science in Early Childhood and Elementary Education from Brooklyn College.

During the past three years, Dr. Ruth has become actively involved in educating other charter school personnel in how to develop standards-based curriculum and assessments. Her school was one of the founding partners of the Tri-County Charter School Partnership, which has implemented three South Florida Annenberg Challenge grants in student assessment and school accountability and two Florida Charter School Dissemination Grants. She serves on several governing boards for charter schools in Miami-Dade and Broward counties, Florida, and is an active member of the Florida Consortium of Charter Schools.

Co-creator of the School-Talk Success Series: *Teacher Talk!*, *Parent Talk!*, *School Board Talk!*, and *Principal Talk!* For more information, go to http://www.school-talk.com.

A Very Special Thanks To:

Our husbands: Tom Cerra and Marty Jacoby, for their unconditional love;
Our children: Alexandra, Frank, Sari, and Scott, for their patience;
Our editors: Vicki McCowan and Paula Wallace, for their thoroughness;
Our designer: Henry Corona, for his continuous creativity;
All of the teachers, students, parents, and community leaders
who have touched our lives;
Our wonderful staff; colleagues; and outstanding
schools; and you, our reader, for reading,
absorbing, learning, sharing,
and growing.

Let us hear from you . . . send us your snapshots. Email Cheli and Ruth at:

Cheli Cerra
Cheli@school-talk.com

Ruth Jacoby
DrRuth@school-talk.com

Other Books in the *School Talk!* Series
by Cheli Cerra, M.Ed. and Ruth Jacoby, Ed.D.

Parent Talk! The Art of Effective Communication With the School and Your Child

This must-have guide for parents provides 52 "snapshots" of just about every conceivable situation than can arise between a parent, a student, and a school and provides clear, simple suggestions for positive solutions. From "My child's friend is a bad influence" to "I don't understand the results from my child's test," it covers all the typical events in a student's school experience.

ISBN 0-471-72013-5   **Paperback**   **www.josseybass.com**

Teacher Talk! The Art of Effective Communication

"An amazing compilation of what to say to parents. This book is a must have for your professional library."

—*Harry K. Wong, Ed.D., author of the bestselling* The First Days of School

An essential guidebook for all teachers that presents effective strategies for handling 52 common situations and simple ways to communicate with students, parents, and administrators. Features worksheets, checklists, sample letters, and more.

ISBN 0-471-72014-3   **Paperback**   **www.josseybass.com**

Principal Talk! The Art of Effective Communication in Successful School Leadership

"*Principal Talk!* provides simple communication strategies and advice to keep teachers, students, parents, staff, and the community in your corner. A must-read for today's educational leader to be successful in today's reform climate."

—*Jack Canfield, co-author,* Chicken Soup for the Teacher's Soul

This user-friendly, quick reference presents 52 "snapshots" of communication issues faced by busy principals and assistant principals in working with staff, parents, teachers, and the community.

ISBN 0-7879-7911-2   **Paperback**   **www.josseybass.com**

School Board Talk! The Art of Effective Communication

For both the aspiring and the veteran school board members, this book offers tips, worksheets, and practical advice to help board members develop and improve communication skills, survive in political office, and make a difference in education. In its user-friendly, easy-to-browse pages you'll find 50 "snapshots" and solution strategies on topics such as: casting the lone "no" vote and surviving, keeping your family in your fan club, building a school board team, handling constituent calls, and conquering the e-mail and memo mountain.

ISBN 0-7879-7912-0   **Paperback**   **www.josseybass.com**

Coming Soon:

Test Talk!: Understanding the Stakes and Helping Your Children Do Their Best

ISBN 0-7879-8274-1   **Available March 2007**   **Paperback**   **www.josseybass.com**